Who Betrayed the African World Revolution?
And other Speeches

John Henrik Clarke

With an introduction by Kwame Nantambu

THIRD WORLD PRESS, CHICAGO

Third World Press
Publishers since 1967

Second Edition 1995
Printed in the United States of America

10 09 08 07 06 05 04   8 7 6 5 4 3

ISBN: 0-88378-1360   (paper)

Cover design by Angelo Williams

Dedication

To Sybil Williams, for all the right reasons.
And in celebration and appreciation of the fact
that you are a part of my humanity
and I am a part of yours.

Table of Contents

Introduction

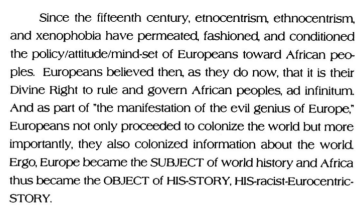

Since the fifteenth century, etnocentrism, ethnocentrism, and xenophobia have permeated, fashioned, and conditioned the policy/attitude/mind-set of Europeans toward African peoples. Europeans believed then, as they do now, that it is their Divine Right to rule and govern African peoples, ad infinitum. And as part of "the manifestation of the evil genius of Europe," Europeans not only proceeded to colonize the world but more importantly, they also colonized information about the world. Ergo, Europe became the SUBJECT of world history and Africa thus became the OBJECT of HIS-STORY, HIS-racist-Eurocentric-STORY.

Eurocentric history, therefore, has deliberately promulgated the myth that Africa was a "Dark Continent" replete with cannibals, savages, and inferior, uncivilized, backward, primitive peoples, devoid of knowledge and culture and possessing evil traits and desires. The erudite Afrocentric historian John Henrik Clarke, however, completely destroys this Eurocentric myth by correctly asserting that:

> Civilization did not start in European countries and the rest of the world did not wait in darkness for the Europeans to bring the light . . . most of the history books in the last five hundred years have been written to glorify Europeans at the expense of other peoples. . ..

Most Western historians have not been willing to admit that there is an African history to be written about and that this history predates the emergence of Europe by thousands of years. It is not possible for the world to have waited in darkness for the Europeans to bring the light because, for most of the early history of man, the Europeans themselves were in darkness. When the light of culture came for the first time to the people who would later call themselves Europeans, it came from Africa and Middle Eastern Asia . . .

It is too often forgotten that, when the Europeans emerged and began to extend themselves into the broader world of Africa and Asia during the fifteenth and sixteenth centuries, they went on to colonize most of mankind. Later, they would colonize world scholarship, mainly to show or imply that Europeans were the only creators of what could be called a civilization. In order to accomplish this, the Europeans had to forget, or pretend to forget, all they previously knew about Africa . . .

For the past 500 years, therefore, the world has been ruled/molded in the image and likeness of Europe. European history now becomes world history and the European experience now becomes the universal experience. One of the primary weapons Europeans have used to ossify, perpetuate, and maintain the myth/Big Lie of European supremacy, invincibility, and originality coterminous with the myth/Big Lie of African inferiority and nothingness is education, albeit, miseducation.

Euro-colonial education was designed to produce people who would participate in the process of colonial rule; people who would participate in the process of their own oppression and in the oppression of their fellow colonialized people (neocolonialism); moreover "colonialized schooling was education for subordination, exploitation, the creation of mental confusion, and the development of underdevelopment," power-lessness and dependency. It also reinforced the "notion of privilege" and the "notion of alienation" (divide and conquer).[2] In other words, colonial and neocolonial education ossified the psychological dependency complex of the African colonized/oppressed to the extent that in the era of what Dr. Clarke terms "flag independence," the African "wasn't preparing to be a sovereign nation" but instead was only "preparing to imitate his slave master's ruling of a nation." *Ipso facto*, Africans not only:

> ...take for granted the validity, truth, and superiority of the culture of the (European) colonizer but (also) assume that the behaviors, culture, values, life-styles, moral preferences, and definitions of morality of the colonized as invalid, wrong, false, or inferior... (Moreover, they) have been infected and conditioned to invalidate and reject their own being and own culture, value and philosophical individuality... (They) tend to evaluate their behaviors in terms of whether or not they are acceptable to the (European) colonizer. (They accept) the colonizer as the standard...(and) crave to be like their colonizers ... [3]

In his book, Dr. Clarke suggests that European scholarship has darkened "The True Light of African History" and as a result, we are brain-dead, brain-damaged, and culturally comatose. What African people need to do as we approach the twenty-first century is to de-Europeanize, de-mystify, de-toxify, and de-brainwash their subconscious mind of this invisible drug called Eurocentric miseducation. In this way, we can relocate our subconscious mind-set to its original locus/reference point—Mother Africa. Dr. Clarke warns that:

> ...We have to realize that education has but one honorable purpose ... one alone ...

everything else is a waster of time: that is to train the student to be a proper handler of power. Being black and beautiful means nothing until ultimately you're black and powerful. The world is ruled by power, not blackness and not beauty . . .

The central theme in Dr. Clarke's book is the sad tragedy of the betrayal of the African world revolution by its own people. He concludes, quite equivocally, that the African revolution was betrayed in three major arenas: in Black America, in the Caribbean Islands, and in Africa itself. He elucidates by suggesting that:

> . . .The main thing needed in Black America was a movement that went beyond religious, political, and cultural boundaries and that unified African people on an all-class basis.
>
> From what we had learned from the Civil Rights Movement, from Martin Luther King, Jr., from Malcolm X and Elijah Muhammad, and from what we knew about the need of common folk in the United States, we could have organized such a movement and related African people to the struggles of the African people of the world, especially Africa, the Caribbean islands, the Pacific islands, and the people of African descent scattered throughout Asia. The Civil Rights Movement could have become the basis of a world movement of African people based on the theories of Pan-African Nationalism. In my opinion, the movement was betrayed by confused ideologist, middle-class fakers and just plain sellouts.
>
> For one moment in history, the Africans in the United States had more attention than any Africans in all the world. They could have used that moment to call attention to the needs of the African people all over the world, not only call for Pan-Africanism, but an African

world community.

The tragedy is not that the Caribbean people have betrayed their aspect of the African world revolution. The deeper tragedy is that most of them have not been aware of it
. . . .

In examining the betrayal of the African world revolution in Africa, Dr. Clarke suggests further that:

...[Kwame] Nkrumah's grammar and the moment in history caused a lot of people to rally behind him who really didn't believe in him. They would ultimately betray him and desert him later on. The United States did not want to see the role model of a well functioning African state in place in Africa. Because if you produce one, you can produce ten. If you can produce ten, you can produce fifty. So the Whites made up their minds between French intelligence, British intelligence, and United States intelligence that nation had to be destroyed. They had to knock off a few nations after Ghana before the independence fever started growing. . . .

It is indeed a universally accepted truism that Mother Africa is the cradle/origin of world culture and civilization and that Africans are the pioneers in science, religion, chemistry, mathematics, education, astrology, philosophy, architecture, agriculture, medicine, iron and steel smelting, the concept of beauty, masonry, moral codes of ethics, etc. It is also a universally accepted truism that "high culture," commerce, and civilization originated along the Nile Valley river, Egypt, in the B.C.E.

Indeed, for the first 110,000 years of human/world history, ONLY African people inhabited this planet earth. No European EXISTED. They were NOT yet created. Yet Eurocentric history, HIS-STORY, has the arrogant audacity to write in their history textbooks that during these 110,000 years, African peoples did nothing, created nothing, contributed nothing, and discovered nothing. African peoples are painted as a do-nothing people. Nothing could be further from the truth. In fact, a correct analysis of history shows that it took Europeans about 20,000 years to defrost, unthaw, and to be metamorphasized from the original advanced global majority African people to a contemporary global minority European people. The bottom line is that we are the ancestors/predecessors of Europeans. We created them. According to R.R. Palmer and Joel Cotton in their book *A History of the Modern World*:

> ... Europeans were by no means the pioneers in human civilization. Half of man's recorded history had passed before anyone in Europe could read or write. The priests of Egypt began to keep written records between 4000 and 3000 B.C. While the Pharoahs were building the first pyramids, Europeans were creating nothing more distinguished than garbage heaps ...

In a fascinating and revealing chapter entitled "The Contribution of Nile Valley Civilization to World Civilization," Dr. Clarke not only debunks the myth of the African "nothingness" but also carefully delineates the dynastical contributions of Africans along the Nile Valley to world civilization.

In looking toward the twenty-first century and the troubling transitional aspect of Pan-Africanism, Dr. Clarke opinions that "it is ironic that the concept of Pan-Africanism was a Caribbean creation and the Caribbean people have made the least use of it." He recalls such Pan-Africanist pioneers as Henry Sylvester Williams, a lawyer from Trinidad, who called a protest conference in London, England in 1900 on the conviction that the "problems of black folk in England were largely based on racism." It was Williams who coined the term Pan-Africanism. Other pioneers include C.L.R. James and George Padmore, both also from Trinidad. Along with W.E.B. Du Bois, these individuals "gave the concept of Pan-Africanism form and substance."

Dr. Clarke defines Pan-Africanism "as any effort on the part of African people to reclaim any portion of Africa that has been taken away, mutilated, misunderstood, or misinterpreted by a non-African to the detriment of Africa." But to this reviewer, the uniqueness of Dr. Clarke's further definition of the historical origins of Pan-Africanism lies in his seminal and path-breaking statement that:

> When I look back at the historical role and the historical manifestations on Pan-Africanism, I deal with the first organized society in the Nile Valley, when the people of the South and the people of the North...came together to form a country now known to the world as Egypt... The unification of the Upper Nile and the Lower Nile was an act of Pan-Africanism, putting a portion of Africa together for the whole of Africa to be together....

This historical Africa-centered connectedness is nothing but genuis at its cultural zenith. As we move toward the twenty-first century, Dr. Clarke's advice is that "we have to understand (that) we have to make certain radical changes in our lives and our attitudes." We have to build from within. We have to reach out to Africa and Africa has to reach out to us. The poignant message is simply: "We are African People, One Nation at Home and Abroad! Only through Pan-Africanism will the African Nation be redeemed." Or in the words of the late Osagyefo Kwame Nkrumah:

> ... All people of African descent, whether they live in North or South America, the

---

Caribbean, or in any other part of the world are Africans and belong to the African nation . . .4

In terms of linkage analysis, this book is right at the cutting edge of a significant time in the history of Africans in America a time when there is serious and acerbic debate in higher education as to the authenticity, viability, and applicability of Afrocentricity. For while there are as many definitions of Afrocentricity based on as many individuals as one may interrogate, Dr. Clarke again provides a unique and path-breaking perspective on the concept of Afrocentricity. In his chapter entitled "The Historical Basis of Africancentricity," Dr. Clarke is quick to apologetically point out that he "do(es) not have a fight with [Molefi Asante]," the putative progenitor of the concept; however, he does have "a fight with his generation" because "his generation has failed to see the latitude and the longitude of the subject that was already old when . . . Asante's parents were born." Dr. Clarke defines Africancentricity as follows:

. . . any sincere effort on the part of
African people (literally or militarily) to regain
what slavery and colonization took away and
to restore the nation as you originally conceived
it to be . . . We are talking about something that
is very broad . . .

A translation or interpretation of this definition immediately brings to the fore the notion that Dr. Clarke focuses on all aspects of the African life experience it represents a multifaceted, historical analysis of the African struggle. As such, Dr. Clarke discusses in detail the revolutionary, literary, religious, folklore, cultural, intellectual, etc., manifestations of Africancentricity. His beef with the word "Afrocentricity" is that "it is a compromise with the world Africa." Dr. Clarke argues that since there is no "fro" in Africa, then from an African historical perspective, there MUST NOT be any hyphenation of the word African. This debate will not end with the publication of this book.

Who Betrayed the African World Revolution? and Other Speeches represents in one volume all the information readers would need so as to ascertain why the African revolution has not occurred throughout the world. The book assiduously discusses the covert collusion between the European powers and their African contemporary house-servants to thwart the revolution. This collusion has occurred both in Africa and the Caribbean. In fact, the only reason why Europeans have been able to rule the planet for the past 500 years is because they have divided African peoples so that they can rule (conquer) them. And they have been very successful. But the book does more than that.

It teaches that the blood that unites us is thicker than the disparate water and culture that separates us. It also teaches that we might have come from the "Old World" (Africa) to the "New World" (Europe) in different European slaveships but we MUST achieve total liberation in the same Pan-African Nationalist freedom boat. The fundamental message of the book is that it is time for African people to stop rehearsing and get the show on the road to total liberation and freedom so that we can ossify our ranks to create our own common Pan-African nationalist Home/Fortress Africa 2100 in order to challenge European Nationalism/Fortress Europe 2100 in the twenty-first century.

KwameNantambu
Kent State University
June 19, 1994

Chapter One

Who Betrayed the African World Revolution?
June 10, 1992

Attorney Alton Maddox opened up an interesting door in history and he teased you by letting you peep inside of that door for a minute. Then he closed the door. I just want to open that door a little wider. Then I'll go to the subject.

He mentioned the closing years of the nineteenth century, the birth of Black politics in New York City, and the United Colored Democrats under Ed Lee who was called the Chief. Ed Lee was the kind of politician we don't have anymore. Ed Lee was the chief bellhop at the old Warwick Hotel where the Tammany bigwigs went for extracurricular activity, not necessarily with their wives, of course.

He knew which room to send the Scotch, the blonde, and the brunette. He knew the dirt on everybody. The then head of Tammany Hall (Ed Coker) was complaining that the Harlem community was Republican. Ed Lee told him the reason why it was Republican. Coker said, "I will not only give you funds to start a Democratic branch in Harlem, I will put a Negro in every branch of government in New York City." This is one of the few promises that was made to us that was almost kept.

The whip that brought it forward was Ed Lee and the United Colored Democrats. When I talk about Ed Lee, I'm talking about a "real" black politician. Most black politicians talk and don't deliver anything but wind. Ed Lee got us jobs as assistants to this and assistants to that. Finally, Ed Lee said, "I'm tired of the little crumbs. I want the big crumbs. I want two judgeships." They told him he had to be crazy.

The Democrats chose a Judge Watson. His son is a federal judge right now. And the Republicans chose one named Toney. Watson was of Caribbean descent and Toney was a Black American. The head of the Black Democrats was a Harvard-educated man from the ghetto who had developed new curse words. His name was Ferdinand Q. Morton. Ferdinand Q. Morton was in opposition to Charlie Anderson who was then Collector of Internal Revenue, First District, Wall Street. He had a ninth grade education. He had enough nerve to go and tell J.P. Morgan, "Mr. Morgan, you are delinquent in your taxes." Morgan said, "Who the hell is that n----," and who gave him an appointment to see me?/[1]

His secretary is supposed to have said, "I didn't think that the Collector of Internal Revenue of the First District needed an appointment./ He got fired from the First District, of course, and started in the Second District. This man had a special nerve. People don't have any nerve like that today. He could open a "nerve/ store and sell some.

Now Ferdinand Q. Morton was the head of the Civil Service workers, and when they appointed him this is Ed Lee's manikpulation; he's asking for the big crumbs now these are first two big crumbs. The white civil servants said they would not work under that n----r. Ferdinand Q. Morton, who had gone to Harvard and could speak all those low languages with a Harvard accent, said, "I know a whole lot of unemployed n----rs who are well educated. If any of you think you're not going to work under me, I can have them down here in your jobs tomorrow morning. They want the jobs, need the jobs, and will take them." The next day those Whites were right in their seats working under Ferdinand Q. Morton. For the next twenty-seven years, that's what they did.

What we're talking about is the beginning of Harlem politics. Now, Ed Lee wanted two judges. Watson and Toney were chosen. When Ed Lee asked for this, he was told you don't have qualified people to be judges. Ferdinand Q. Morton, who made some of the choices, told Watson, "You just go down there and judge something. You're just as good as all those wops, kikes, and everything else."

Watson was from the Caribbean, where he had seen his people perform as judges. He had seen them as schoolmasters and in other petty power arenas. Toney had never had that experience, and he didn't even believe that they were going to accept him. So, according to the Harlem mother. When he came back, Ferdinand Q. Morton had some new curse words for him, and he became a judge. That's how we got our first two judges.

These two men Ed Lee and Ferdinand Q. Morton opened the door for the career of Adam Clayton Powell, Jr. They created the first Harlem political Renaissance. There's a literature on it. There's a literature on everything on it. There's a literature on everything, you now. Roi Ottley, in the Book, *New World A Coming*, has written on it. Gilbert Osofsky, in his book, *Harlem: The Making of a Ghetto, 1890-1930*, has written in detail on it. The book, *Harlem on My Mind*, has information on it, including pictures. Also, if you forgive the modesty, the Introduction to my book, *Harlem: A Community in Transition* and another book, *Harlem, U.S.A.*, has a capsule history of this political emergence of the Harlem community.[2]

I have emphasized this because history sometimes tells you where you've been, in order to tell you where you are, so you can estimate where you still have to go. Because I'm a classroom teacher, when someone throws a subject out, I want to broaden the subject. I want to tease you just a little more. I'm going to open the door a little wider. Now, I'm going to close the door to that subject and go on the subject for tonight.

We first have to define what exactly is a revolution. Our crisis today is that we do not seem to understand that a revolution means a complete change. In a revolution you do not patch an old society. You replace an old society. When a society has grown old, weak, fat, and flabby and fails to serve its people, the conscious role of those who have suffered from that society is not to prop up that society, but to change that society in such a way that it will never be the same again.[3]

When that society was originally built on your sweat, your life, the tears of your mother and father, you not only have the right to change the society, you have the responsibility to do so. First, let's look at the revolution of the nineteenth century in the African world and find out who betrayed that revolution in the twentieth century. You cannot fight to become a part of the apparatus of your slave master. If you do, you will re-enslave yourself. Your job is to destroy that apparatus.

Early in the nineteenth century in Africa the chattel slavery system (another form of slavery was turning into the colonial system. Remember slavery is never abolished. Slavery is transformed. Now it is computerized. Only the slave can destroy slavery. You cannot destroy slavery by becoming a part of your slave master's cultural incubator.[4]

You have to understand what happened to you in this transfer from one society to another. You developed a cultural incubator that was collective and homogeneous by virtue of being collective. The people who enslaved you put you into another cultural incubator which lacks humanity and used religion as a utility to move things from one place to the other. They could not even afford to mend democracy or Christianity. The very existence of that power and the way it existed was anti-Christian and anti-democratic. So they had to preach about it in order to try to convince themselves that they believed in it.[5]

Now when you go back to the original culture that you had

before the interference, you didn't preach about it. You lived it out. When you created a religion, you didn't say, "I am my brother's keeper." If you are genuinely your brother' keeper, you don't shout it out. You just keep him. You live out the culture. However the enslaver proclaims the culture and betrays the culture. When you get confused between the incubator that created you and the one that enslaved, you have a problem which is our present-day problem. How did that problem come about? We have misunderstood the nineteenth century black activists and black ministers. We have misunderstood their connection in the African world of the nineteenth century.

When that chattel slavery system began to disappear because of its being unwieldy—and not because of the goodness in anyone's—heart you will discover (if you read it well) that most of the White abolitionists were fakes and phonies. Granville Sharpe said, in his own literature, "Though I am a Christian, I have found it difficult to put my hand in the hand of another African Christian and call him brother." He was talking about Equiano, the greatest author of the African Christian slave narratives. Equiano was more Christian than he.

Yet when we look at Granville Sharpe's life—while he was against slavery as an unwieldy system—every legislative act against child labor in England he voted against. Every act to improve the lot of women he voted against it. When the British wanted to use colonies as a dumping ground for unwanted women in the population, he voted for it. He had no humanity for even the Englishman of his own kith and kin.

This man with the greatest reputation as a British abolitionist was a liar and a faker. The Africans began to understand this fakery early in this nineteenth century and started a series of wars to break the British and French hold on their countries. In South Africa, a series of Zulu wars would last 254 years. They began with the entry of the Dutch in 1652 and ended with the last Zulu War in 1906. In West Africa, a series of Asante wars started in 1800 and ended in 1900 with the last Asante War being fought by a woman, Yaa Asantewa, who was exiled. That war was finally broken by the famous West Indian regiment. That requires a whole lecture so I won't get into that tonight. If I got into that lecture fully, I would need a six-pack and six handkerchiefs.[6]

There were wars motivated by the spirit of African Islam. This is difficult for you now because you're so hung up with Arabic Islam, you don't know that there's another Islam. African Islam began to set these wars in motion in West Africa against the French—Sekou Toure's grandfather, Samory Toure; in the Sudan a man named Muhammed Ahmed and called the Mahdi (which means the holy man). He was the one who fought with his famous "fuzzy wuzzy" warriors who were not Moslems. However, he unified the whole Sudan.[7]

Farther to the South, a war was started by another devout Muslim, Mohammed bin Abdullah. He was called the "Mad Mullah" of Somaliland. In North Africa, a war started against the French by Abdul Krem continued with another African who did not lose power until 1956, Glaoui Pasha.[8]

My point is that all Africa was at war throughout that nineteenth century. In the Sudan, we have the British going back to avenge the fact that the Africans had driven them out of the Sudan. They went back with a superior army under General Wingate. This was reported by a young British reporter, Winston Churchill. His was one of the finest jobs of war reporting since Caesar came home for Gaul. It's called The River-War. The same Churchill would report on the last of the Zulu wars in a book called A Roving Commissioner. He would recall that Africa had out-generaled some of the finest military men in Europe, and these Africans never wore a store-bought shoe or heard of a military school.[9]

This nineteenth century war in Africa would set the twentieth century in motion. Near the end of the nineteenth century, missionary Africans began to appeal to the conscience of the colonialists only to discover that in a game of power, conscience is absent from the makeup of the European.

Now in the Caribbean, early in the nineteenth century, they had already fought some of the best strategized slave revolts in history. Haiti had become free. Jamaica had fought harder without becoming free. There were revolts in South America such as Palmares and the Berbice Revolt in Guyana. These revolts happened before the American Revolution. The revolt in Palmares gave the Americas its first republic, before the American revolution. Yet, these Africans got left out of history because they weren't on Europe's side.[10]

Haiti furnished a haven for South American activists, especially Simon Bolivar. Once he established South American freedom, he would turn on the very Haitians who had helped him. In dealing with the Caribbean revolts, Caribbean people—even today in their self-congratulation—misunderstand this aspect of their heritage. They do not understand that if they've had the most successful slave revolts of Africans outside of Africa, it had nothing to do with them being braver than other Africans.

Caribbean slave masters bought in large lots and kept the lots together. They thought they could work them better that way. They were right. But they could revolt better that way, too. They had linguistic continuity, cultural continuity, and joy continuity. Therefore, when that one beat the drum, the other one over there knew what the drums were saying. They could maintain a system of communication. In the United States, where they bought in small lots, broke them up, outlawed the drum and outlawed their religion, they destroyed their loyalty system.

In the final analysis, the Caribbean people did less with the loyalty system than anyone else. But they did have it. They did have the finest example of an African cultural continuity of any people living outside of Africa. It was preserved to a great extent in Brazil and other parts of South America, but it almost disappeared from the Caribbean islands except briefly with the Rastas, who sometimes became rascals, who misused African nationalism. It is unfortunate that in some parts of the Caribbean islands, Rastafarianism became a fashion and a fad with no connection to the original African nationalism. Some Rastas, who exploited Rastafariansim for personal use, are still doing so. When you go to the beaches of Jamaica and see Rastas roaming the beach, satisfying these unfulfilled white ladies, I think some of them missed the point. If Rastafarianism had a mission, this is not part of its mission.

Quaddafi, in sending some Libyans to Europe for educa-tion, was supposed to have said a very crude and correct thing. He said, "I am sending you to Europe to get technical education to lift up Libya, to come home and be good Muslims and good Arabs. Remember, you cannot make a good Muslims and good Arabs between the legs of a European women." Now that's cruel and crude when you should have the right to go with anyone you need to. But have you asked, "Who will your daughter marry? What is the future of your daughters?/

I was asked recently in a lecture in Canada by a girl whose parents are divorced, her father is black and her mother is white. She stood up and asked, "Well, what is going to happen to people like me?" I said, "I don't have any answer." But I remember once making this remark, "If you take a clear glass of water and put a few drops of ink in it, you can't use it as ink and you can't drink it as water."

I maintain that confusion set in during the twentieth century when people spoke of the Maroon Revolt, but they spent the greatest amount of their time aping British mannerisms. They spoke of Mansong, Tacky, Gordon, and Paul Bogle, the great Jamaican rebels. But they were trying to give themselves a verbal revolutionary heritage while living conservatively. Colonized Jamaica is the most stratified along color, class, and economic lines of any nation in the Caribbean. This kept it from becoming the great island nation that it still can become if it moved beyond its own mythology. This is the nation that created a Marcus Garvey and denied a Marcus Garvey. Yet, when we look at the golden opportunity that community sent forth to the world, Trinidad gave the African community the three major Pan-Africanists: H. Sylevester Williams, C.L.R. James, and George Padmore. The irony of this revelation is that they could never unify Trinidad, let alone the African world. Trinidad also gave the African world the brilliant political scientist and historian, Eric Williams and the Civil Rights activist, Stokely Carmichael, now known as Kwame Ture.[11]

The Virgin Islands gave the great internationalists, Edward Wilmot Blyden and Hubert Henry Harrison. From Jamaica again, the great consolidators like Marcus Garvey and J.A. Rogers who introduced the idea of accentuating the role of the African in the history of the world. Rogers spent most of his life digging up this information from libraries, documents, and files all over the world. He died broke and today most Jamaicans don't know that J.A. Rogers was a Jamaican.

Isn't it ironic that from the Caribbean islands would come a literature of African awakening and African awareness? Yet you would go there today and find no awareness of consequence. "Everybody trying to be those things most unlike themselves ... feeding grist into other people's mills," as Edward Blyden said in his famous Inaugural Address at Liberia College in 1881, over 100 years ago. "Nothing comes out," he said, "except what has been put in."

Therefore, when they came down to the end of the nineteenth century, they began to discover that their boasting about emancipation coming in the Caribbean islands thirty years before it came to the United States was so much rubbish. It was a fake over there and it was a fake over here. Both of us were still slaves.

Yet the Pan-African Congress of 1900 called for all of us to forget these divisions and become one people. Marcus Garvey said we had, "One God, One Aim, One Destiny." When he said, "Up, up you mighty race, you can accomplish what you will," he didn't divide them based on islands. He didn't say those for Georgia. He said all of you. Up, up you mighty people, you can accomplish what you will. He was trying to restore belief in one's self.[12]

During the whole of the nineteenth century in the United States—that first half was more magnificent—we saw the bringing into being of men like Frederick Douglass and Henry Highland Garnet, and during the end, great preachers like Henry McNeal Turner. On the eve of the Civil War, we saw African people fighting for themselves, not waiting to be freed. The Civil War wasn't about the defeating of slavery anyway. If you think any White people fought four years over you, then that wasn't water you've been drinking. They were fighting to unify the United States.[13]

Now this brings us to that second half of the nineteenth century in the United States: the betrayal of Reconstruction. The period of betrayal from the Reconstruction (1876) to the emergence of Booker T. Washington is called the Nadir, the period of our lowest ebb. By 1895, the Whites had gotten tired of dealing with a multiplicity of black leaders, so they chose one for us. They chose and anointed Booker T. Washington. They gave him publicity and they gave him the means. Some people were for him and some people were against him. In spite of the fact that he was "chosen," he did some innovative things in education which are still good for us. However, because we didn't like some of the things he did, we turn against some of the useful things we still need.[14]

Thus, all of us came into the twentieth century. The Caribbean islands came angry and fighting over constitutions.

The Africans came during the end of the warrior/nationalist period and the beginning of the missionary-trained, political activists. In this country, we were beginning the end of the physical struggle and the beginning of another great struggle.

We have the great black journalists: T. Thomas Fortune, William Monroe Trotter. We were in the midst of the Du Bois period, the Booker T. Washington period. There was a fight for education. There was a fight to build independent black institutions and a fight over their name. All of this as we came with us into the twentieth century.

The political and cultural transition of Black America from 1875 to the emergence of Booker T. Washington and the decline of Blacks in elected politics is ably described by Professor Rayford W. Logan of Howard University in his book, *The Betrayal of the Negro*. There were some betrayals and some institutional building concurrent with institutional decline. Black America began to be plagued by some misconceptions of the body politic of the American nation, that was not cleared up to this very day. Africa was nearing the end of its 100 years of anti-colonial wars. The slave revolts in the Caribbean islands were over. Throughout the African world activists were now petitioning and appealing to the alleged Christian conscience of our oppressors. With these illusions, we came into the twentieth century.

This is the African Revolution that was the preface to the twentieth century revolution that we betrayed. Why did we betray this revolution? We have to look at the years in Africa, the United States, and the Caribbean islands. Because who was in charge, who were the spokesmen in the main during those years? They were people who thought our greatest hope was to be like our oppressor instead of destroying our oppressor. Though they fought for a new society, they would model that society on the corrupt and dying society of the oppressor.

When the Africans began to ask for a new society, they

were asking for an African-dominated society. But most of the Africans asking the questions were trained by the oppressor. They had forgotten their own methodology of rule, and so the methodology of running a state was borrowed from the oppressor. The oppressor never develops the methodology for the liberation of the slave. Powerful people never educate powerless people in he kind of special education they need in order to take the power away from them. [15]

The aim of powerful people is to stay powerful by any means necessary. If they have to buy up the wheat, they but up the wheat. They know something which you have illusions about: the meek will not inherit the earth. The strong will inherit the weak, and status quo will remain the same. The earth will always be ruled by strong people. And if you want to rule it, become strong. Stand on your own turf.

When we look at those years in Africa after World War I and before World War II, the people that they looked for to bring a government into being were nearly all trained in European schools. There was nothing wrong with them being trained in European schools. So were the Japanese. But the Japanese got proper instructions before they went to the European schools: "Your job is to come back and make a Japanese nation that can defy those people, out-produce those people, and remove the humiliation inflicted by those people." They came to American schools with their little cameras and they took pictures. Americans were insulted by the picture-taking. Everybody was saying, "Oh, those silly little Japanese." By the time they went home, they could make everything they took a picture of.

If they took a picture of a train, they could go home and make a train. The African didn't do that; the African was too busy being the imitator instead of an innovator. He wasn't preparing to be a sovereign nation. He was preparing to imitate his slave master's ruling of a nation. And his slave master's apparatus would never fit him. The revolution was being betrayed before the revolution ever occurred. I don't mean just in Africa. The same thing was happening in the Caribbean.

People were moving into place who would play a color game, an economic game, and a class game. No one was speaking directly for the ordinary people who worked and labored. Everybody with an education had their nose in the air. The common people had no advocate. Until the common people have an advocate, you have no revolution.

After World War II they were fighting for constitutional government and land reform because the British had Crown lands (reserved land). Anything to keep the land out of the hands of the people. They would pull this trick all over Africa. They couldn't exactly pull it in West Africa. Land tenure would remain intact thanks to a man named Casely Hayford. Hayford, from Ghana, wrote an excellent book on it, *The Truth about the West African Land Question.* Jomo Kenyatta wrote a good book about the East African land tenure—very few people have read it—*Kenya, Land of Conflict.*[6]

When you take away a people's land, you take away their nation. You take away their birthright. You might as well take away a woman's womb and tell her, "Go ahead and have some more children." It's impossible. No land, no nation. The land was being lost in Africa and the land was being fought over in the Caribbean islands. They made a better fight over it in most cases, and some of the land was being returned to the people. They did have some redistribution of the land. But the elite who participated in the redistribution of the land ended up buying up some of the land. They exchanged a British land-owning aristocracy for a black island-owning land aristocracy. Power changed faces, but power did not change methodology. Again, power remained out of the hands of the people.

In 1945, Kwame Nkrumah—who had been in America—was back in England to attend the Pan-African Conference in Manchester, England, along with Padmore. This was the theoretical beginning of the African Independence Explosion. In 1947 he was called back home to be secretary to Joseph B. Danquah, who headed the United Gold Coast Convention. Nkrumah pulled the young people out of the United Gold Coast Convention and founded the Convention People's Party. It was under the banner of the Convention People's Party that he led Ghana to independence.

Nkrumah's grammar and the moment in history caused a lot of people to rally behind him who really didn't believe in him. They would ultimately betray him and desert him later on. The United States did not want to see the role model of a well-functioning African State in place in Africa, because if you produce one, you can produce ten. If you can produce ten, you can produce fifty. So the Whites made up their minds—between French intelligence, British intelligence, and United States intelligence—that nation had to be destroyed. They had to knock off a few nations after Ghana before the independence fever started growing.[17]

As the independence fever started growing, the traitors grew just as fast. The Joseph Mobutus, the murder of Patrice Lumumba, Moise Tshombe, the African Uncle Toms. Then Africa was in shambles. There were different cleavages in Africa based on who was a Moslem, who was a Christian, and who was an Animist. Freedom isn't about religion. Freedom is freedom. You can be free under any of them or a slave under all of them. Religion should never have been part of the issue. But they were hiding behind it.

Now you have the Caribbean Federation concept propagated, but falling apart because of inter-island rivalry. Norman Manley was of the opinion that Jamaica would have to end up paying taxes for some of the smaller islands. He had some questions about Jamaica's role in the Federation. While this talk was going on, the best intellect of the talking group was Eric Williams. Finally Eric Williams went home and discovered he had some oil. He told the Federation to go to hell and went "his/ way. So the concept began to fall apart.

In the United States, a fight for equal pay for teachers was converted into a fight for equal education. What called the larger issue to the attention of people previously unaware of the significance of the situation was the Montgomery bus boycott and the emergence of Martin Luther King, Jr. King emerged into a situation which was created before he arrived. He was drafted and placed into a situation. A very common man named E.D. Nixon was really in charge, and he chose Martin Luther King, Jr. to head the movement. Nixon was a common, ordinary man, Pullman porter-type. He not only split infinitives. He created some new ones[18]

All of us have to remember that English is not our mother tongue and if we want to chop it up once in a while, that's our privilege. Just don't chop up Yoruba, Igbo, and Hausa. These are our mother tongues. We should speak them correctly when we get around to speaking them. As for English . . . well, we weren't born with it. It was forced upon us.

I'm trying to point that out because we sent students to school without giving them a nation-mission, when they came out of school they didn't understand the nature of their commitment to us. So in the Caribbean they become "English." In the United States, they become "I'm an American. I'm an American." The only way that you can find out whether you're an American very easily is to try to catch a cab downtown. If you can't pass the "taxicab test," forget it. The cab driver doesn't care where you're from. That bigoted cab driver is a better Pan-Africanist than most of us. He looks at all of us as the same.

Once the Civil Rights Movement began, it moved by leaps and bounds. It took on a different meaning after the Emmett Till case. Seriously study the impact of the Emmett Till case and the events leading up to the March on Washington, where the movement began to stagnate. The Whites threw out some money—almost a million dollars—between six organizations with an agreement that they'd all work together. Working together killed their creativity and soon the money was gone. Nothing was happening. Then came the killing period—Kennedy, then Malcolm, then King—the politics of assassination. The same kind of politics of assassination is happening in Africa and the Caribbean: the politics of exile and banishment.[19]

Keith Henry has written a Ph.D. thesis called, "Tigers Abroad and Meek Moses at Home: Conservatism, Radicalism, and the Caribbean Mind." He deals with the conservative factor of the Caribbean mind at home and the radical factor away from home. It's a phenomenon that deserves at least two or three more Ph.D. theses. My radical orientation in my early years in New York City came from Caribbean radicals to a great extent. On the street corners of Harlem, stepladders of Harlem—Raphael Powell, J.A. Rogers, Richard B. Moore, Petion and all these groups were fighting for the independence of their respective islands.

Some of the best debates I ever heard were calling attention to the writings of some of the finest Caribbean scholars who are forgotten now. I never hear anybody mention T. Albert Marryshow of Grenada and his *Cycles of Civilization*. He was one of the few radicals that stayed on in the Caribbean. He did not migrate. He died there. I saw his son in Barbados. He has totally disgraced his father. He's nothing but a white woman chaser. That's a tragedy that pops up in the most unusual places.[20]

In conclusion, in the United States during the Civil Rights Movement, young people who worked for ten dollars a week and wore blue jeans opened up the door for a generation of Blacks to go to schools that they never would have been able to go to. A generation later, those same Blacks began to look down their noses at the very people who had opened those doors. Some of them began to advocate the closing of the doors in the face of those who had opened the doors. An army of traitors appeared in the whole African world. They are paid traitors. Some of them are in government. Some of them are called chiefs. Some of them are heads of states. Some of them are on the periphery. All they have gotten out of it have been Mercedes-Benzes, some Swiss bank accounts, and the premium of the European women (which is very easy to get).[21]

The years between the March on Washington and the assassination of Malcolm X and Martin Luther King, Jr. need to be seriously studied. These were the years when a lot of people throughout the African world were selfishly betraying the ideas of the Black revolution and making peace with the enemies of African people the world over. These fakers and traitors had fought very little, if they had fought at all, and announced through their actions that they were tired of fighting. The African revolution had been betrayed on all points.

Our mistake is that we did not take the Japanese approach. This is where you line up the young men and say, "Sociology for you, engineering for you, oceanography for you." You understood what went into the making of a nation and you trained at least ten men for every item, and you did not say "please." A case in point is that the Japanese, formerly an agrarian nation, by 1905 was technically efficient enough to kick the Russians in the behind and demand respect in what is called the Sino-Japanese War. People began to talk about "The Yellow Peril" or "the Yellow Danger."

We shouted "nation-time" too soon. We shouted "nation-time" before we understood what a nation is. To have a nation you must know everything that goes into the maintenance of the nation. If you shout "nation-time" and you do not produce the safety pin that holds your child's diaper together, then you have shouted prematurely. You aren't ready for nation-time. If you've got to depend on someone else's food to eat and are producing none for yourself, then you are not a nation. A Mercedes-Benz will not make you a nation. A limousine will not make you a nation. You're just an inadequate fool with a chauffeur.[22]

The next time, if fate is kind enough to present us with a next time, we'd better know what makes a nation. We'd better deal with our traitors. I advocate the re-establishment of the old African Blood Brotherhood with an accompanying sisterhood—an internal security force. We won't take you to the white man to be punished. We will punish you so well that we won't have to do it too many times. When you do wrong and see us coming, you'll run to the white man because his punishment will be much less than ours. If you talk nation-time, you've got to think nation-time. There is no salvation for this people except some form of Pan-African nationalism.

You've got to stop worrying about those "little specks of dust" in the Caribbean where the slave ships put you down and worry about where slave shops took you from. The common denominator must be Africa. This does not rule out your being proud of what particular island you came from. However, the priority over this is that we are all African people. If there are a billion of us on the face of the earth, we better learn how to speak with a single voice. We must reach out to the Africans in the Pacific Islands, India, and Sri Lanka. Maybe a third of all Africans in the world live outside of Africa. Africa might have the lock to the future, but I think we have the key. We've got to get that lock and that key together. We have to deal with Africans who now have their noses in the air and are saying, "I am the descendant of a pure African and you are the descendant of a slave." If you are that stupid, you are the slave, mentally.

We have to build a world where we will not only refuse to be a slave, but we will refuse to be a slaveholder, also. We will build a common humanity for ourselves that will benefit the whole world. But first and foremost, we will build it for ourselves, for our children and their children still unborn. However, we have to deal with people who betray our revolution and we have to identify them and punish them in such a way that others would have second thoughts about betrayal.

We have to find partners for our revolution. I suggest you start with yourself and a mirror and don't move until you like what's staring back at you. Then unify with those people throughout the world. Recently through every lecture and question & answer period, this keeps popping up—the controversy around interracial marriage and interracial dating.

I have said he is the descendant (the great-grandchild) of the same people who brought you over on those filthy ships. You betray these Africans who suffered by laying down with him, when no people have made amends to us for what happened to us. Maybe after they pay us compensation over and above their national treasury and help us to restore our sovereignty, I might think about it as a conversation. But who told you that the people you look like weren't good enough to sleep with? If you've got a problem about who to sleep with, then you've got a problem with the people who produced you.

How did your mother look, and how did your father look? You mean to tell me they were wrong in bringing you into the world the way you look? Why do you assume that you have to go to the former slave master to get a mate? Have you no respect for your image? No people will be free until they love themselves so much that they rise above slavery, even at the risk of death. We have to stop shouting to the world about being black and beautiful, because if you believe it, you wouldn't have to shout it. You would walk into a room and everybody would know that beauty is there because you are there.

I have often said we can change the world if at first we change ourselves. We must remember the world is not ruled by blackness or beauty. It's ruled by power. Black and beautiful means nothing unless, ultimately, you are black and powerful.

In conclusion, the African revolution was betrayed in three

major arenas: In Black America, in the Caribbean islands, and in Africa, itself. There is now a need to examine, in some detail, the nature of this betrayal if we are to recover form it and prevent its recurrence in the future.

Black Americans emerged form the Second World War somewhat cynical and frustrated over the Jim Crow treatment of black soldiers, over the lack of jobs in war industries, and the continuation of the system of segregation. Many black soldiers had fought a war to make the world safe for other people without finding any safety for themselves and their respective families. The fight for equal pay for black teachers was gradually turned into a fight for equal education. This fight led to the Supreme Court decision of 1954 outlawing discrimination in schools. In our assessment of this event, we immediately went wrong because we did not sit down in community after community, organization after organization, and strategize. Instead we celebrated. We made no assessment of our still prevailing enemies. Those who erected the Jim Crow system were not going to change overnight, if at all. The Ku Klux Klan and other racist organizations had no plans to change at all. Too many Black Americans interpret integration as meaning amalgamation. They began to dismantle or neglect sustaining institutions in the black community. There was a decline in entrepreneurship, a general decline in black store ownership. The black community was partly self-contained with its own barbershops, tailor shops, restaurants, small but clean hotels that kept the community intact, free of total white dependency.

Some Blacks were so joyful about being able to use the same facilities as Whites, they neglected their own facilities to the detriment of the community. The approach of the NAACP, that had rendered great service in the legal arena, was disastrous in the social arena. Our children were bussed into white schools to create an alleged racial balance without either white or black student being explained how to get along with each other. Many white teachers and students who resented this sudden move, psychologically cut some of our students to pieces and scarred them for life. Both Blacks and Whites went about integration the wrong way. The how and the why were not explained ahead of time.

The Montgomery bus boycott of 1955 and the emergence of Martin Luther King, Jr. solidified the basis of the Civil Rights Movement. The embryo of this movement was set in motion by the Freedom rides, defying Jim Crow and buses, the Sit-in Movement at lunch counters, and the demand for equal education on the college level as well as the primary level.

Leaders were coming forth faster than people were coming forth to be led. Some were able. Some were interesting charlatans. Because most of them spoke well, sometimes it was difficult to distinguish one from the other. The Movement was centered in the South with strong influence in the North. Because of the mass media and white liberalism, the Movement was beginning to get world attention. Some Whites abroad genuinely sympathized with the plight of Black Americans. Others pretended because of some reasons unrelated to Black Americans. They disliked the United States. The important point here is that the Black American Movement in the U.S. was beginning to get world attention. At the center of this attention was the personality of Martin Luther King, Jr.

The unfortunate murder of Emmett Till, August 1955, heightened the drama and the seriousness of this movement, and increased its nationwide followers. The organization of CORE (Congress of Racial Equality), SNCC (Student Non-Violent Coordinating Commitee),[20] and the Southern Christian Leadership Conference comprised the main part of the consortium that projected the Civil Rights Movement. The NAACP was the legal arm of the Movement and remained firm in this position until the aftermath of the March on Washington, 1963. The creation of the Anti-Poverty Program siphoned of some of the most able personalities in the Civil Rights Movement. The Urban League was the employment arm of it. Some unemployed college graduates and executives without jobs in the Civil Rights Movement now had well-payiing jobs in the Anti-Poverty Program. Some former activists, who previously sang, "We Shall Overcome," got the impression that they personally had already overcome. Some of them toned down their criticism of what they called The Establishment and joined The Establishment. The Civil Rights Movement was in the process of dynamic change. The common folks and the students were still boycotting, still picketing, still going to jail. Some members of SNCC were wearing blue jeans and making ten dollars a week. Massive suffering still went on in spite of the fact that some of the original members of the Movement had quit the fight.

The March on Washington was a high point in the Civil Rights Movement. The world attention that was given the Movement gave some people the illusion that the Movement was moving forward when, in actuality, in effectiveness it began to decline. The March on Washington was controlled by forces outside of the Movement. Six large black organizations, including the major civil rights organizations, were told to come together to cooperate and were given considerable large sums of money. Because each one had their own style of operation, the attempt to come together ended in stagnation and a decline in their effectiveness. Gradually they drifted apart. At the March on Washington, Martin Luther King, Jr. made his most famous and least effective speech. In my opinion, it was a golden opportunity, tragically missed. He had a dream, but he did not have a plan. While he had the attention of the world, he was expected to announce a dynamic plan for change, not a dream. It might or might not be realizable. Although it was not noticeable at the time, the effectiveness of Martin Luther King, Jr. began to decline after the March on Washington and the "I Have a Dream" speech. The people were turning more and more to another voice that was stronger, clearer, and more dynamic. It was the voice of Malcolm X, who was calling on Blacks to believe in themselves again, to understand their enemy and to lose their fear of the enemy. He was also calling on them to reclaim their manhood and their womanhood and once more to have the confidence and the skill to rule nations.

Martin Luther King, Jr. had no difficulty with adversaries, black or white, so long as he was preaching non-violence. When he began to criticize the war in Vietnam, the misuse of the resources in the U.S., and began to advocate the Poor People's March on Washington, black, white or otherwise, he was on a collision course with the powerful forces in modern-day history. In my opinion, the decision to kill Martin Luther King, Jr. was made at this moment.

The assassination of Malcolm X on February 21, 1965 and the assassination of Martin Luther King, Jr. on April 4, 1968 removed the two greatest spokesmen for black liberation in the twentieth century, with the exception of Marcus Garvey. Now without specific direction, Blacks could retreat into middle-classism. Some hid behind color gradations, fraternities and sororities, and other social organizations. The common folk, who at least had the illusion of having champions in Martin Luther King, Jr. and Malcolm X, felt that they now were without a champion. The movement led by Elijah Muhammad was still functioning, though it was never a part of the Civil Rights Movement. It was a pseudo-religious uplift movement whose mass appeal was limited. The main thing needed in Black America was a movement that went beyond religious, political, and cultural boundaries and that unified African people on an all-class basis.

From what we had learned from the Civil Rights Move-ment, from Martin Luther King, Jr., from Malcolm and Elijah Muhammad, and from what we knew about the need of common folk in the United States, we could have organized such a movement and related African people to the struggles of the African people of the world, especially Africa, the Caribbean islands, the Pacific Islands, and the people of African descent scattered throughout Asia. The Civil Rights Movement could have become the basis of a world movement of African people based on the theories of Pan-African Nationalism. In my opinion, the Movement was betrayed by confused ideologist, middle-class fakers, and just plain sellouts.

For one moment in history, the Africans in the United States had more attention than any Africans in all the world. They could have used that moment to call attention to the needs of the African people all over the world—not only to call for Pan-Africanism, but an African world community.

The uniqueness about the Caribbean aspect of the African world revolution is that it was continuous until near the end of the nineteenth century, when it became more verbal than military. The uniqueness about the people of African descent in the Caribbean islands is that the organized revolt of the Africans away from home started in the Caribbean islands. The first recorded revolt of the African people against slavery was a revolt in Cuba, 1527. These revolts were continuous throughout the Caribbean islands, parts of South America, and Brazil. Africans in the Americas, especially in the Caribbean islands and in South America, were fortunate enough to use African cultural continuity as a part of the revolt. A large number of slaves in these areas spoke the same language and came from the same culture areas in Africa. Those who did not understand the same tonal language understood the same drum language, a means of communication. In the U.S., through sale and re-sale, broke the Africans' cultural continuity and their loyalty system.

In Brazil a large number of Portuguese men married African slave women with the permission of the Church. These women became free and were the mothers of the first families of Brazil. This kept down some slave revolts but not all of them.

Some of the most successful slave revolts in what is referred to as the New World were in Brazil. Because of the Maroon revolts and others, the Caribbean people could keep the military aspect of their cultural continuity intact for more than 200 years. Haiti and Jamaica furnished more economic resources for Europe than any colonies in the Americas. That is the reason why absentee overseers pushed the slaves beyond human endurance to make still more profits. The most continuous and the most successful slave revolts were in Jamaica and Haiti. By the middle of the nineteenth century these revolts were declining and the period of negotiation had set in. At that time England had created a second army in Jamaica and some other islands. They had created generation of mixed breeds—bastards who had questionable loyalty. Some enjoyed a status over the Blacks, but not as good as that of the Whites. Another factor to be taken into consideration is the creation of the Caribbean freeman: the British and other colonists the British had brought over, wheelwrights, boat menders, and repairers of sugar mills and their equipment. These technicians, who had no appreciable status in their home countries, found that they had status away from home in a sea of African faces over and above any status they had at home. Their whiteness alone gave them status. Life on tropical islands was too rich for most of them. Some became exhausted by saying yes to every temptation. Some drank themselves to death. Some gambled and lost plantations. Some returned to England. The main point here is that the Africans learned the basic technologies the white technicians had brought to the islands to practice. The status of these Africans improved because they became essential to the maintenance of the plantation system. As blacksmiths, they often made the cutlass for the sugarcane and, when not being closely watched, they made stabbing knives and secretly gave them to the slaves in the field.

After the middle of the nineteenth century, the mulattos in

Jamaica and some of the other islands wanted to legalize their special status. They couldn't be white. They did not want to be classified black. In Jamaica, when they could not get this special status, they threatened to join the Blacks. Some joined the Blacks. Some became spies among the Blacks. But they never gave up the idea of special status. This could be the beginning of the idea of stratification in Jamaica along color, economic, and classlines. By 1865 the Africans on Jamiaca and the other islands began to discover that the emancipation which had come thirty years before was another form of slavery. Most former slaves were now working on the same plantation for a small salary and with the responsibility of buying his own clothes and furnishing his own home. They discovered that they had changed their position without changing their condition. In the first half of the nineteenth century, the Caribbean freemen, especially those in Jamiaca, had made contact with the free black activists in the United States. Prince Hall, who grew up in Barbados, had founded the first Black Masonic Lodge that he called the African Lodge. Peter Ogden of Antigua had participated in founding the lodge now known as the Odd Fellow. John B. Russwurm, also a Jamaican, had been one of the editors of *Freedom's Journal*. He later went to Liberia as the governor of one of the provinces, as the founder and editor of *The Liberian Herald*, which is still in existence.

Also in the middle of the nineteenth century, Robert Campbell of Philadelphia, formerly of Jamaica, accompanied Martin Delany in search of a place for settlement in Nigeria a few years after the settlement of Liberia. Cooperation between African American freemen and Caribbean freemen continued until after Emancipation (1865) and down to the end of the nineteenth century.

The most notable Caribbean figure to go to Africa in the middle of the nineteenth century was Edward Blyden. Blyden tried to build a three-way bridge between Africa, the Caribbean islands, and Black America. But he was refused entry into American schools. He returned to Liberia where he became president of Liberia College and on another occasion Liberian ambassador to England.

My point here is that humane dialogue existed between African Americans and Caribbean Americans throughout most of the nineteenth century. We did not think of ourselves as a separate people with separate problems. At this time the color factor did not interfere with our relationships.

Near the end of the nineteenth century, a Trinidadian lawyer, H. Sylvester Williams, founded the Pan-African League. He called a Pan-African conference in London in 1900 and set in motion the Pan-African congresses that would ultimately be the basis of the African demand for independence. The Caribbean Federation concept came into being concurrently with the African Independence concept. This was a merger of ideas from Africa, from Black America, and from the Caribbean.

Again, it is ironic that the concept of Pan-Africanism was a Caribbean creation and the Caribbean people have made the least use of it. The finest minds and personalities developed in the Caribbean islands have not found comfort in trying to live out their lives in the Caribbean islands. Marcus Garvey was a failure twice in Jamaica. There is no extensive Garveyism in the Caribbean islands today, except among the Rasta, whose adherence to Garveyism would be superficial. The books of Edward Blyden, in most cases, are not in the libraries of the Virgin Islands where he was born. The political conservatives in the Caribbean islands and the color conscious permanent residents have found no place for the Caribbean radical thinkers.

Noone of the three major Pan-Africanists from Trinidad (H. Sylvester Williams, C.L.R. James, and George Padmore) are widely known in the island of their birth where they grew to early manhood. Walter Rodney of Guyana, one of the finest thinkers the Caribbean people produced in the twentieth century, taught in Africa, Jamaica, and in the U.S., and had a difficult time finding employment at home, where he was subsequently assassinated. Richard Moore of Barbados returned to his home island after forty years when he was old and ill and subsequently died. T.A. Marryshow of Grenada, one of the few Caribbean writers who stayed in the Caribbean, is unknown to this generation of people.

The tragedy here is not only that the Caribbean people have betrayed their aspect of the African world revolution. The deeper tragedy is that most of them have not been aware of it.

Caribbean people in general, both at home and abroad, though they deny this with voices like thunder, are in retreat from their blackness. Most of them are quick to tell you about their English blood, their Scottish blood, without reference to their basic blood, which is African. Too many times they are not only divided along color lines, they are divided along gradations of color. I have found that Caribbean people who have been colonized by England have a fascination for Whites that is downright sickening. Though the Carribean people created a clear revolutionary heritage in the fight against the brutality of slavery by bringing off some of the most successful slave revolts the world has ever known, including the most successful in Haiti. However, presently too many Caribbean people still act as though slavery did not occur in the Caribbean islands at all.

All too often, Caribbean people, African Americans, and Africans engage in conversation that is a comparative study of oppressors without any judgement against oppression or oppressors. Sometime what they are saying, in essence, is that my oppressor was less severe than your oppressor; therefore, my status is higher than yours.

What is forgotten here is that if you are against any form of oppression or slavery, you are against all of it and its variations based on time, condition, or who's practicing it. If you are against all evil, you never choose the lesser between two evils. There is a common denominator that should unite the entire African world. All African people were oppressed. All African people were conquered and colonized by Europeans and Arabs one way or the other. You are either against all of them or you approve of all of them. Sometime to make a comparison is tantamount to comparing the venom from two poisonous snakes without understanding that both poisons will kill you.

In the 1950's the whole of the African world was on the march one way or the other. The rise of anticolonial movements in Ghana affected people in the Caribbean islands and in the United States. This was an opportune time to structure a union of all African people based on the interests they had in common—a single enemy, mainly with its origin in Europe and Western Asia, mistakenly called the Middle East. The intellects of the African world missed a golden opportunity in not using this occasion to call for a union of the African people of the world. Because many of the ideas about Pan-African nationalism, African awakening, and the reidentification with Africa were started by Caribbean activists, idealistically they should have joined African and African American activists in calling for cooperation in the formation of an African world community.

One of the most significant parts of this African world community, unified by pan-African world nationalism, could have been a strong federation of Caribbean states. This was not brought about because of the overwhelming influence of the former colonial master, who was still manipulating Caribbean people behind the scene and sometimes overtly on the scene. They did not feel economically and politically strong enough to make this important decision. Had this decision been made and had a true federation been founded or developed, there could have been a Caribbean defense force, economic union, and a federation of educational systems in the Caribbean on all levels.

Caribbean scholars could have thrown out the British, Spanish, Dutch, French, and Portuguese textbooks used in their schools and developed textbooks more relevant to Caribbean people in their relationship to the African people of the world. A federation of this nature might have been in a position to prevent the tragic invasion of Grenada (October 25, 1983) and Panama (1989). These invasions, stripped of their rationale and military romanticism, were nothing but one colonial master taking over from another.

There is a small library of writing on the subject. Here I refer you to a few important pieces from the writings of C.L.R. James: *A History of Pan-African Revolt*. Washington D.C.: Drum and Spear Press, 1969, *The Case for West-Indian Self Government*. London: Hogarth Press, 1933; *Party Politics in the West Indies*. San Juan, Trinidad; C.L.R. James (approx. 1962); and "Federation," a lecture delivered to the Caribbean Society, Kingston, Jamaica in November, 1959.

In the final analysis, it must be clearly realized that Caribbean people of African descent are part of the total African world. And they have no long-range future outside of the ultimate participation in an African world community. Their former slave masters and their former colonial masters have no formula for their salvation. The large presence of European blood in their veins will not change their predicament one iota. The white father that created a large number of them has made no room in his house for any of them. Caribbean people who are in retreat from African people because of their degree of European blood are retreating into oblivion. There is no future for the Caribbean islands until there is a collective realization that these islands are a part of the universal house of Africa. All Caribbean people, irrespective of color gradation and European parentage, either have a permanent home in this house, figuratively speaking, or no home in the world at all.

The embryo of the African side of the world revolution against slavery, colonialism, and oppression began in the 1700's

B.C. with visitors from Western Asia and later invaders who had colonial aspirations. The collaboration between the initial visitors and the invaders, referred to in history as the Hyksos and sometimes as Shepherd Kings, set in motion an assault on African culture and ways of life that would continue in different forms until this day. The African recovery from this initial assault renewed the energy of North and Northeast Africa, basically Nile Valley civilizations. Africa enjoyed a thousand years of peace before another invader, the Assyrians, now called Syrians, came in 666 B.C. Like all invaders, they did Africa more harm than good and opened the door for still another invader in what is now Iran, then referred to as Persia, in 550 B.C. A lot of the soldiers of this invasion married into African families and began the mulattoization of Nile Valley cultures to the point that some of the former invaders, now married to African women, joined their respective wives in a complaint against the invaders from Persia. While in Africa, some of the soldiers switched loyalty because of their relationship to African women and some because of their admiration of the great achievements, spiritual and material, in the country that they had invaded. The weakness that set in by the disruption of this invasion opened the door for the first truly European invasion, the invasion of the Greeks by Alexander of Macedon, 332 B.C. The Greeks did not understand African culture and tried to alter it and make it their own. Alexander was bold enough to acknowledge that Africa was the home of the Greek gods. His stay in Africa was not long. Still with a hunger to conquest, he and his army would move toward mainland Asia where he dissipated too much of his energy and subsequently died.

The significance of the above referenced note is in a statement that I have repeatedly made to both students and general audiences over the last fifteen years: Africa has been under siege for over 3,000 years. The enemies of Africa have either been at the door, in the house, or in the African's bed. The late William Leo Hansberry of Howard University has called Africa "the world's richest continent," which indeed it is. Africa has always had, and still has, abundant resources and energy that other people want, think they can't do without, and don't want to pay for. This is the basis of the more than 3,000 years Africa has been under siege by foreigners.

Africa in general, especially Nile Valley civilization, has had three golden ages. The European assault on Africa that started the slave trade and subsequently colonialism came at the end of the third golden age. The first two golden ages unfolded in and around the Nile Valley with the Nile River being the world's first great cultural highway. The third golden age had its beginning in or near the Niger River and brought into being great independent African states and empires like Ghana, Mali, Songhai, the Hausa States in Northern Nigeria, the Ibo States in Eastern Nigeria, the Yoruba States in Western Nigeria, only to name some of the most outstanding. Dissension in the coastal states of West Africa and an invasion of the inner coastal states, called the Western Sudan, from Morocco in North Africa disrupted more than a thousand years of African independent state building and permitted the slave trade to spread into the hinterlands of West Africa. In the meantime, the Arab slave trade was already more than a thousand years old. The Arabs were slaver traders before the rise of Islam. There are many documents and references on this point. The best immediate documentation on this point is *Slavery in the Arab World*, by Murray Gordon. African people in general are so romanticized by Western organized religions, they have forgotten that all of them have participated in their enslavement.

The invasion of Africa in the fifteenth and sixteenth centuries, as well as the establishment of the slave trade and the colonial system that followed was an assault on African culture and all ways of life developed by the Africans themselves. This assault would continue until the latter part of the eighteenth century when chattel slavery became an unwieldy labor system and was transformed gradually into colonialism, a more sophisticated form of slavery. The African Revolution that I am referring to here was developed in wars all over Africa in order to oppose this new slavery. In North Africa the Turks, Mamelukes, and the last phase of the Ottoman Empire were grudgingly in retreat. This opened the door for various European powers to stake claims in North Africa concurrent with staking claims in Western Asia. When a large number of Africans and African kings, mistakenly referred to as "chiefs," realized the nature of European encroachment on their socereighty, they did not sit down to negotiate. They picked up their spears and their shields and went to war. These military encounters would last over a hundred years. This African revolution in the nineteenth century was betrayed in the twentieth century because European-trained Africans in leadership or clerkship to the colonialists did not transfer information about the previous anti-colonial conflict that was military to their anti-colonial conflict that was only verbal. While Africa produced mainly European missionary-trained radicals who confronted the European and settler governments in Africa, they appealed to the conscience of the European without knowing it was the lack of conscience and concern for the African's way of life that brought these invaders to Africa in the first place.

There is a need to look briefly at some of these African revolutionists of the late nineteenth and early twentieth centuries who confronted the Europeans and tried to hold onto the sovereignty of their lands.

In Morocco, El Hadj El-Glaoui made every effort to hold onto the traditional structure of Morocco. He was the last of the great rulers of this part of Morocco that included the city of Marrakesh.

Osei Tutu of Ghana headed the reorganized Asante State of Ghana that remains intact to this day. The Akan people fought a number of wars with the British in an attempt to hold onto their traditional culture. The last war was fought by the Queen Mother of Asante, Yaa Asantewa. Further along the coast of West Africa personalities like Samory Toure stopped the French movement inland in their attempt to establish what was later to be called French Equatorial Africa.

Wars in North Africa, the Ashanti Wars in West Africa, the wars in Upper West Africa against the French, the Zulu wars which lasted in some form for over two hundred years, and resistance against the Germans in Tanzania, Togo, the Cameroons and Southwest Africa were all revolts against European encroachment on the sovereignty of African nations. These were wars led by brilliant nationalists of the Moslem faith, the most noted being Mohammed Ahmed (the Mahdi) of the Sudan and Mohammed ben Abdullah Hassen. The last of the Zulu wars was fought after the Boer War in 1906, by Bambaata. Great women had also given splendid accounts of themselves in these African wars of resistance, mainly Queen Nzingha of Angola and Nehanda of Zimbabwe. This is the African Revolution of the nineteenth century that in many ways was betrayed in the twentieth century.

The last of the struggles to colonize all Africa is reflected in the Italian assault on Ethiopia in 1896, when the Ethiopians successfully turned back the first Italian invasion. In the closing years of the nineteenth century, when some European powers thought they had not received their proper share of Africa, they sat down at the Berlin Conference and the rest of Africa was partitioned. After the partition (1884-85), all Africa was under some form of colonial rule, directly or indirectly. Liberia has always been considered an American colony.

Because of her basic cultural homogeneity, Ghana, referred to as the Gold Coast by the Portugeuse, gave birth to some of the most articulate radicals. I am referring to the works of Casely Hayford: *The Truth about the West African Land*

Problem, Ethiopia Unbound, and *Gold Coast Native Institutions.* The book, *Toward Nationhood in West Africa,* written by another Ghanaian, lays out a blue print for independence still to come, though it was a generation away at the time. Joseph B. Danquah in his writing tried to preserve the best traditions of Ghana while emphasizing Africa's relationship to the concept of right and wrong before they had any knowledge of Christianity, Islam, or the Hebrew faith. Because Danquah was a scholar with a comprehensive view of history, he knew and strongly inferred that the spiritual elements that went into the making of organized religions, came out of Africa in the first place. The mainly European-grained comissionary-educated Africans who led Africa into independence did not evoke the spirit of using the literature of liberation already created by Africans to chart the way of the Africa still to come. Many of them were European-trained messengers and clerks and apologists in retreat from their tradition of culture and ways of life. This in the twentieth century was the ultimate betrayal of the African military struggle of the nineteenth century. Many of these new Africans were individuals who had broken away from the cultural moorings of the African society that had produced them. In their action, they were Europeans in black-face. In no place in Africa did they bring into being a purely African state based upon African ideas and the African concepts of religion, culture, commerce, and trade. They seem to have forgotten that the nation-state, with its tight borders, was not an African creation. The African functioned best in the territorial state with numerous cultures and religions coexisting side by side. In order to rule the Africans, the Europeans felt called on to put these different cultural entities against each other and to create a fragmented colonial Africa that was not dismantled after independence. Because of these border restrictions and cultural divisions, many Africans became strangers to each other. Indirectly Africa had been recolonized in the name of independence and

Africans had participated in the recolonization of themselves. This, again, was the ultimate betrayal.

In summary, what have we learned in the years between the independence of Ghana and the present time, and what can we do about it? Until the independence of Ghana (March, 1957), the Pan-African idea, born and developed away from Africa, was a motherless child. In March, 1957, the day of Ghana's independence when Nkrumah announced to his people, "At last the long night is over. Ghana, our beloved country is free forever," Pan-Africanism, the motherless child, had found both a home and a parent. What all Africans should have done at that moment, in Africa, the Caribbean islands, and the United States is to develop an operation and definition of Pan-African nationalism that could be flexible enough to be applicable to all Africans everywhere. At that point there was a need to seriously plan the structure of an African world community that would bridge all religious lines, cultural lines, and geographical lines. In this 500 year struggle against slavery and colonialism, all Africans have had one enemy, no matter the geography, the religion, or the culture. A redefinition of Pan-African nationalism and the development of the concept of an African world community would have given all of us a bridge where we could stand and communicate with one another. That would have been the common denominator of Pan-African nationalism.

Because our origin is Africa, our political heartbeat should be in tune with Africa. No matter where we live on the face of this earth, we should proclaim ourselves an African people. That is our nationality, no matter what nation we were born in and what nation we choose to live in. This is the ultimate vindication of the betrayal of the African world revolution. We must be bold enough to look back and re-echo the words of Marcus Garvey: "One God, One Aim, One Destiny." Then we must say to every African person on the face of the earth with the shadow of a doubt about him or herself in the future, "Up,

Up you Mighty Race, You Can Accomplish What You Will."

The above statement needs some examination and some clarification. By One God, I do not mean that all African people on the face of the earth should be bound to one spiritual system. We can adhere to many different belief systems while having the same basic objective. The fight for African liberation can be carried on under any belief system.

What I mean by One Aim is that all African people one way or the other should be committed to African liberation, unity, and preservation, irrespective of religious, cultural, or political commitments.

By One Destiny, I mean the unification and the development of the African people. Any place is of value to African people every place in the world. I am not talking about a clan or a cult. This can be achieved without African people encroaching on the lands of other people or infringing on the rights of other people.

Professor Hazel Reid, in her short book by the same name, has asked for A Ritual For: A New Liberation Covenant. In a collective way, I am asking for the same thing. Because we engage in so much ceremony without substance, I am asking that we add some substance to the ceremony of becoming free of alien domination and staying free of the same.

I had the following reaction to Professor Reid's call for a ritual that is repeated as follows:

> In this Ritual for a New Liberation Covenant, Hazel Reid has raised some fundamental questions about the religion of the oppressors as an instrument for the liberation of the oppressed. All over the African world there is the search for an ideology of liberation and for a new concept of religion that will compliment that ideology. In our attempt to use our oppressors' "Christian" religion as a liberating force, we are dealing with contradictions in

definition. If our oppressors were really "Christians," they would not be our oppressors, for the act of oppressing others is un-Christian. It is clear that if Christianity is going to be a doctrine of liberation for us, we will just have to recreate this religion according to our own needs and feelings; or we will have to create some other ideology. Further, if we are to understand this New Liberation Covenant with God, we will have to ask ourselves some hard questions, for example: What is there in us of strength and weakness that made us accept our oppressors' distorted concept of a religion which we created in the first place? Why did we buy the story of a heavenly compensation, with the promise of milk and honey and long white robes, while others, at our expense, were building a heaven on earth for themselves with our labor?

We have found very few clear solutions to our problems in the realm of Western history, sociology, and the sciences. It may now be the time to look into the possibility of finding some solutions through an understanding of ritual in our search for a New Liberation Covenant; and in doing so professor Reid is quite in order, and her call is one that is long overdue.

In calling attention to the African world revolution and its betrayal, I am asking African people to reclaim those vital assets that have always been a part of their history, culture, and politics. As a people, we have always been revolutionary, creating change and adjusting to change. Today as we stand at the crossroads of our history in particular and world history in general, we might have to strategically step backward in order to move forward with a clear definition of ourselves. We began by restoring our self-confidence and our image of God as we originally conceived him or her to be. This view is revolutionary. We are revolutionary people. Professor Williard Johnson of

M.I.T. has reminded us that we can change the world if at first we change ourselves. When we look back at the river valleys: the Nile, the Niger, the Congo, the Volta, the Limpopo, the Zambesi and especially the Nile, along these rivers we brought into being at the dawn of history the concepts, the social thought, and the methodology that man would later call civilization. This was a social revolution that changed the world. With the restoration of self-confidence, we can boldly say to ourselves and to the world, "If we did it once, we can do it again."

Chapter Two

The True Light of African History
April 1983

Before getting into the lecture, I'd like to call your attention to the fact that we are not the only people searching for our history and its true light. I saw the picture, "Gandhi." Technically, it is a great film. Historically, it is a great error. I noticed how carefully they left Africans out of the film even though his fight started in South Africa. They left the confrontation with African people out and the scene where he is thrown off the train is an historical error.

What they did was put him in the car with the Blacks. He resented that. When Whites needed more space later in the journey, they made the Blacks clean the car, then they put all of them off out next to nowhere and Gandhi understood then that he was no higher than the lowest Black in South Africa.

He still could not tune into Blacks. The East Indians still have not tuned into them today. Because we haven't dealt with brown racism, it has hampered our ability to deal with white racism. It also hampers our ability to deal with ourselves.

Now, if you just saw this in its true light, you would see Gandhi having a quandary with himself about why he couldn't associate with Whites, why he should associate with Blacks. This has been documented time and time again. I went back and checked the information on this for my own sake.

Gandhi founded the United Colored League, a league which consisted of all the people in South Africa (excluding the Blacks). That didn't work. Then he founded the United Natives League which included the Blacks, but the high-minded arrogance of the Indians offended the Blacks and the United Native League wouldn't work. This would have been great drama had they put it on film. Now, the Indians face up to the great African nationalist of his day, John Tengo Jabavu.[1]

When facing up to the Africans of that day, while he fought for the rights of every man, he had not fully accepted the Africans as men. He did not fully accept all men as men until he went to India and had to face up to the problem of the Untouchables.[2] It was then he began to face himself as a bourgeois aristocrat who was, to a degree, looking down his nose at other Indians. Then he had to deal with himself.

When I saw this I saw a film that, if your look at it well, is really an apology for British colonialism. You'll notice that they put in the "good" British characters who are in effect saying, "We weren't quite so bad?" When they dedicated the film to Lord Mountbatten I said, "Uh-oh, I'm going to see colonialism served up again."

After Gandhi left for India, the United Natives League was influenced by an East Indian named Dr. Abdurahman and his organization, the African People's Organization. Dr Abdurahman, in order to get the government to remove the restriction from the Indians of carrying the identity pass, agreed to turn his back and let the pass be carried by the Africans. Once more the "guest in the house" had turned on the host. To this day the East Indians in South Africa hold themselves aloof from the Africans in South Africa. Africa will be free, maybe sooner than we think, then the African is going to have to ask some questions about the "guest in the house."

The one thing we should learn about this, once we make

a film about the true story of African people, we're going to have to do it ourselves. Because looking at a film that is "technically" well done, historically it is a disaster. They never told you the story about Gandhi and his fasts. All the fasts were fakes.

Years ago when I made a speech at Bank Street College on what Martin Luther King, Jr. did not learn about Mahatma Gandhi, two ladies came in the middle of my lecture and led me from the podium. They sad, "That's enough." I was going to do an analysis of King and Mahatma Gandhi as a master politician. He was a politician and he had a violent alternative waiting in the wings just in case the nonviolence did not work.[3]

I was trying to get across that when Gandhi told Indian people to take off all those British clothes and go back to the spinning wheel, entire British industries went bankrupt. What I was assuming (in comparing) that had Martin Luther King, Jr. told African Americans to take off Western clothes, go make clothes from your own mills, make your own shoes, he could have started an industry in this country of black people supplying themselves with those things that they need to sustain themselves. He did not learn this.[4]

To Gandhi nonviolence was a tactic. Gandhi had said this. To King, however, it was a way of life. The thing about a tactic is that once it has served its purpose, you throw it away. Just like you throw away an orange when it has no more juice. It has served the purpose, out it goes.

What I am trying to get across is the crisis in history is a worldwide crisis. If brown people cannot tell the true history of their relationship with us, you know full well white people can't afford to do it either.

In preparation for this talk, because I've got more time now than I've ever had in my life (recovering from an illness), I had time to think, rethink and reread things that I've read before. I've had a lot of time to listen to the voices of my fathers. I've had a lot of time to think of the people who trained me.

I had teachers. I didn't just emerge out of nowhere. Those teachers took me in hand and trained me, free of charge. I was thinking about what they pointed me to: the great events in the history of our people before the Europeans. How did we handle justice? How did we handle right and wrong?[5]

I was thinking about my early years in Ghana when I witnessed a trial of no significance because the amount of money involved was less than ten dollars. The man said he'd give back the ten dollars to the other two men who did his work while he goofed off with a lady. The two men said, "No." They wouldn't take it. I said to myself, "What is the trial about?" It went on and on and on.

Finally it ended when the wife pleaded with the other two men to work with him again as their partner. She said, "His mouth was bitter now." That means he's broken his promise. "Work with him again so his mouth can be sweet." So he can be trusted again.

I went back to Accra trying to figure out what the trial was about. I asked the great Ghanian figure, Joseph B. Danquah, who treated everybody like a school child, including Kwame Nkrumah who used to be his student. He said, "John, stop talking like a Western jackass. That trial had nothing to do with money." Then he went in his library and pulled out a little pamphlet, wrote his name on it (I still have the pamphlet) and handed it to me.

I went down into his library and read. He said, "When you understand it, come up. My wife will have dinner. Stay there and read it until you understand or you don't get your dinner." When I came up I said, "Dr. Danquah, the trial was about honor and obligation." He said, "Yes, John, my wife will serve dinner now. You understand." African society is governed by honor and obligation. And we arrived at what was right and wrong before we know a European existed.[6]

What I have been trying to do with this time that I have now is to look back and see our history in its true light, to see the philosophical basis of our history. How did we govern ourselves? We made promises and we kept them to each other. There was no stealing because everybody had everything and everything in the society belonged to everybody in the society. We had no class because there was no such thing as a class in a properly run communal society. We illustrated and displayed among ourselves more "communism" than there is in Karl Marx's *Das Kapital*.

I think when you have to formalize a law that means somebody doesn't believe it. In African society when you tell a brother to take care of the wife of his deceased brother and their children, there is no law that says he must do this. Yet, he won't refuse to do it. It is in the realm of custom. We must study custom.[7]

Once in Ethiopia where some white women were championing the rights of Ethiopian women, the European women were saying, "We should have laws saying this. We should have laws giving us equal rights." An Ethiopian woman professor, Dr. Jean Selassie, was laughing at the whole thing. She leaned over to me and said, "These Western women do not understand that if they wrote out equal rights into law, equal rights is all we would get. But, if we left it in the realm of custom at home with the shades drawn and the door closed . . . I get more than equal rights."

When you come to a society if you know its law without knowing its customs, you do not know that society. So I've been going back and looking at certain things that emerged out of the humanity of African society, because that was the custom of the society and not necessarily the law. The custom was stronger than the law itself.[8]

I've heard many Africans say, "I would not do this because it would reflect badly on my whole people." So the custom of your whole people becomes your "personal" keeper. Therefore, to see your history in its true light, you have to see your culture and your customs. You have to know: how did you govern yourself before these people came in with their artificial laws? If the European believed in law, he would not have had to write it down.

There are certain things that people do not do because it is not the right thing. The elders arrived at this decision and you were reared to "do the right thing." You don't have to make a doctrinarian book saying, "Do the right thing."

Also, in listening to the voices of my fathers, I have been looking back at a lot of the old people in my own family in looking at how Africans solved problems without the assistance of Europe at all.

I looked at the story of Akhnaton, the great social reformer, a pacifist who believed in peace so much that he disbanded the army. He told the colonized nations who were under Egyptian rule, "If you want to get out from under Egyptian rule, you may do so." They subsequently did. As a reward for this, they began to protect Egypt. Egypt's former colonies gave her more protection than those same people when they were under Egyptian rule.

It was a move of wisdom. Who would have the humanity to banish the army of an empire? I was trying to deal with what Martin Luther King, Jr. did not learn about Mahatma Gandhi. With a better sense of our history and customs, King could have helped turn the African world around by calling attention to what we still could do ourselves.

I illustrated this with a very gruesome example which I think prompted the smiling ladies to come and lead me from the podium saying, "That's enough." I said that if all of us decided that our dearly beloved ones when they are deceased would only be buried in coffins made by Blacks, we would have to open ten coffin factories at once. Think about who controls the coffins in America now. The Mafia controls the coffins you bury people in.

Who controls the coffins in Africa or Jamaica? It is the local carpenters who are not racketeers. They can turn out some beautiful ones. You can order them. They'll have them ready. Tell them what kind of decorations you want on them. Local carpenters.

Why, then, do you go to a racketeer to pay ten times more than what it's worth to bury your dearly beloved one? It is because you have not tuned into how Africans operated and took care of each other before they became so dependent on Europeans and then asking them to do so.

When I look back, I see the Ethiopian emperor Abreha (800 A.D.). At the time he proclaimed the independence of the Ethiopian church (even pulling the Coptic Church away from Egypt), he proclaimed to his people and to the world as well:

> We seek no advice form Rome or Greece. With the affairs of Europe we will have nothing to do. In the future we will decide who will be King of Kings, Elector of God and Lion of the Tribe of Judah. We will order mercy; and dispense justice in the name of the true god and the true religion.

Remember, Abreha headed an Ethiopian Christian nation that was Christian in an Ethiopian way before the Europeans touched African Christianity that far south. He was leading at a time when Ethiopia had just saved Islam. Ethiopia went on not only to be an independent Christian African nation that is still here, it went on to testify by building the great churches at Lalibela which possess some of the finest Christian architecture in all the world.

When the Crusades occurred in Europe, Ethiopia did not join the other Christian nations on the Crusade. These fools think they were looking for the Holy Grail. The Ethiopians said, "We never lost it. You may be looking for your Holy Grail. We never lost ours because ours is right here in the mountains of Ethiopia."

I'm trying to say that we created classless societies and communal societies far more communist than anything in Russia long before Russia emerged as a modern nation. If we want a revolution, then we can look back at revolutions we've already fought successfully, in as much as we've fought more than other people in the world. If we want men of peace, if we want examples of how to govern a peaceful government, we can go back to look at our own men of peace.

We can look at Akhenaton who thought so much of life that he would not crush a flower. He thought so much of life that he would not permit a single human being to be killed. He restored the concept of monotheism (the oneness of God) to the world. When there was a revolt against his doctrines, he left the city, went south, built another city, raised flowers and appreciated his beautiful wife, Nefertiti, sometimes thought of as his cousin.[11]

Once again in 1600 A.D., a king came to power in what is now Zaire. Then it was the Congo. The King was the great Shamba Balongongo. He banished warfare and sent his men to learn of all things: how to crochet. He had men learn knitting and needlepoint. Better that than to go around killing people. Put down your spear.

He thought so much of his ministers that he would never argue with a minister in public for fear he might hurt his feelings. If he had a conflict with a minister, he would take him out of earshot so his family and the public would not know there is an argument between the minister and the head of state.

We have produced men of peace down through the ages and if we wanted peace we could go "home" and get an example of how to be peaceful. If we wanted a revolution, we can look at our own life and get revolution. No revolution in the Americas was more significant that the Haitian Revolution, a successful revolution with slaves.

The Berbice Revolution, in what is now Guyana, happened over 100 years before the American Revolution. The American Revolution was no more a revolution than the Civil War was a civil war. It was just a fight between two branches of white people over who should hold power. It was no more a revolution than the French Revolution was a revolution. It was a conflict between the upper bourgeoisie and the lower bourgeoisie on who would control who and the slave trade at the time.

We have brought off genuine revolutions. I am tired of people coming to us condescendingly "teaching" us about revolution. I am tired of this conflict between people imposing religion and doctrines on us, assuming we are an ignorant people who never created the same things even better.[12]

In regards to the Marxists, I think there's a conflict that has to be solved. There is confusion between the Karl Marxes and Groucho Marxes. I think the funny people are getting confused with the serious people. Personally, I've got nothing against Karl Marx or the Founding Fathers who created the Protestant white nation. I have enough sense to know that Karl Marx wasn't speaking to us. Neither were the Founding Fathers.

When we go back to our own fathers, we go back to the momumental black revolutionists and social reformers here and in Africa (especially the nineteenth century). Then we are beginning to see people who spoke directly to us. We have spent too much time assuming that someone planned something for our benefit. If anything is planned for your benefit, you will have to do it yourself.

We seem to think that the conflict in the world depends upon whether we choose Russia or the United States. I am against both of them. I am not against them because of their ideological systems. I am against both of them because they intend to rule over us by any means necessary. The rule of one is just another exchange of slavemasters. Please remember the

Russians are not in Afghanistan distributing flowers or singing Easter psalms. They are distributing death.

I've been trying to point to the fact that Abreha in this message to the Ethiopians (telling them that we will do for ourselves) was advocating a system that we now call non-alignment. He was advocating this way back then. When King Kwame Ansa of what is now Ghana told the Portuguese in 1482, "It is best that we see each other infrequently. Familiarity may spoil our friendship." The King ended his message with these beautiful words:

> The sea is forever trying to conquer the land and the land with equal stubbornness is forever trying to conquer the sea.[13]

It is best that two people who meet on a road of conflict, if they decide that both of them want to win, the only way they can have peace is to part company. One of them would have to win and one of them would have to die if the conflict continues.

I emerged from the sickness and vicious attack on me from the Left, not as a Conservative, but more radical, revolutionary and more to the Left than ever. However, I will be to the Left in context with my own people's fight for freedom. And that fight will take precedence over everything else because that is the all-consuming passion of my existence.

I will continue to participate to a degree in international forums as I've always done. But I will know where "home" is. I will never be confused. Ultimately, whatever problem I have, or whatever destiny I have will have to be resolved within the context of "home."

I have been told, "The hoodlums and the gangsters of Harlem are on your side. They have passed the word to the other hoods, gangsters, and thugs that if anybody touches you, they'll have to hide. You won't even have to protect yourself. The Underground has said that you better not be touched." Then I walked away with the consolation that in my treatment and in my relationship to all of our people on all levels, including the gangsters, I have behaved with a humanistic dignity that commands their respect.

What continued to pull me back to health are the echoes from within this group (First World Alliance) and my own community. Also, about two weeks ago, the main numbers banker for the community (who would kill you in a minute if you interfered with his business and wash you away if you disturbed him) blew his horn when I was down on the street. I said, "Who is that?" Then he stopped and told me who he was. He said, "What a pity it is for you to be with that cane. I know what happened to you, and I know the forces that came down on you. Don't you worry. You'll get well. And we'll take care of you. Need any money?"

I said, "I'm managing all right." He said, "Need some . . . let me know." Then he opened the door and gave me his card. He said if any one or anything bothers with me in this community, let him know. "Don't you fight. Call me." He opened the glove compartment of his car and there were three .38 pistols. He smiled at me and said, "Remember, Professor, I've passed the word that nobody had better lay a hostile hand on you." Then he went on his way.

Now what did I owe him? I've had no relationship with him. I would occasionally meet him at the newsstand. I speak to him. However, there was an element of respect in my relationship with him that when he told me his business, I did not condemn him. I asked, "Were you around when Caspar Holstein was around?" He said, "I'm not that old."

Caspar Holstein split part of his take with the community and used part of the money from the numbers to send Blacks to college, especially if they came from the Virgin Islands. In fact, we shared so beautifully in his profits that no one dared call him a racketeer in his day. He lent $11,000 to Marcus Garvey. But that's another lecture. Garvey never paid it back. I have a letter that Garvey wrote him, calling him "that great Race man who knows and serves our needs."

In looking back and trying to understand the voices of our fathers, we are looking back at the wisdom dispensed by black people over the years—by African people everywhere—and to study how we survived in the conflict of coming in touch with other people without making an agreement with other people.

We came out of a society that did not write out agreements. If we said something verbally, our mouth was sweet. That meant we could be trusted, and we didn't have to write it into law. If anybody sees you creating a pattern, they know it's yours. You don't have to copyright the pattern because nobody's going to steal it. Once more we see honor and obligation running through the totality of our society and the totality of ourselves.

I went back to looking at the works of Willis N. Huggins, one of my teachers who went to Geneva during the Italian-Ethiopian War. He was one of the founders of the Ethiopian world revolution. I remembered some of the things that he told me then that have influenced me as a teacher, especially as a person preparing to teach. He said, "Make a map leading into the area where you intend to go. In case you don't get there, those who will come after you will know how to get there. You will have a map to tell people where they are going." I thought about this quite a lot. This is why I make so many notes.

I can come here and deliver this lecture without making a single note or a single minute of preparation. Why did I spend two days making notes and going over things I already know? I was making a map. In my files, these notes will be filed so that students and other people coming after me (when sleep comes down to sooth my weary eyes) will know precisely how I prepared for a lecture. That's a map. It's a map of what I did on a certain day. It's a map of what I took up on a certain day. It's a map of what I took up on a certain day. It's good example in teaching.

Then again following the voices of my fathers like Schomburg, he said, "Study the life of your masters. Then you'll know why your history was left out of world history." Then he said, "Anybody who must leave a whole people out of world history and declare that people inferior, must be inferior themselves." He often said, "Inferior things normally fall into an inferior position and stay there without any coercion or anything. Ask yourself why it takes so many laws, so many police, so much brutality to keep us in a position less that other people, and we still bounce out of it and start over ... if you didn't have the energy to survive?" Keep asking this question. That is what I'm here for this evening, to ask the questions as to what has happened to us in history and why did it happen.

Why is our Holocaust, which started five hundred years ago still active? Why did we, a people who came against our will to the Western world to do labor, multiply while our "masters" began to disappear? Why this furious jealously? Why this war in schools against black males? They are the ones who can sire and women can bring to birth some who may change the world. They wish to kill the embryo of our children who are still unborn.

With our "tropical" temperament, we are facing the "iceman." It will never work. I'm not saying that you yourself must have an iceman temperament. But you must have a "realistic" temperament. You must stop looking to Europe and to Europeans for any form of salvation. The European mind never developed anything that did not have as its intention the facilitation of Europe's control over the world. That is all Europe intended for its philosophy/ideology to be.

Now this becomes clear if you examine Marxism and the

role of European Christianity in colonialism, if you examine the Russians in Afghanistan, if you examine how the communists destroyed the great black-built trade union movements in Southern Africa because they couldn't control them, if you examine the roles they're playing right now thinking that the world had forgotten that and cottoning-up to South Africa, hoping that they will have an "in" when South Africa is eventually free . . .

One thing you must deal with in dealing with the iceman, you must concede that in matters of power, he is more practical than you are, because he deals without sentiment. You say that this is happening to a human being and your human dignity lets you impose considerations on people that save their lives. He doesn't have these things to think about at all.

I've been trying to say to you that we must continually look back in order to look forward. We must draw from our own revolutionary existence—our existence is a revolutionary existence—the example we need in order to exist in the world of tomorrow. Let's look back at our most revolutionary period in this country, the nineteenth century.[14]

We need to go back and read David Walker's *Appeal*. We need to see what a great strategist Nat Turner was when he made that fake "confession" and told that White man, Thomas Gray, absolutely nothing. Read "his/ confession. He ain't saying nothing. Everytime he tells you about somebody, they're dead, too late to catch that one. Anybody who escaped, he didn't use their names. If there was somebody mentioned who was supposed to have fought with him, he would say, "I never knew what happened to him."

He never said a mumbling word about who helped him plant the revolution. He never said that he had a wife who was the secret keeper of the Nat Turner revolt. All the documents, maps, places where guns could be found, the information was not kept on Nat Turner. It was kept on his wife. He would never admit that he had a wife, because he knew they would find her and hang her like him.

When they asked him standing blood-stained in tattered rags with chains, "Aren't you sorry about what you did?" He said in essence, "This is the consequence of revolt. I might die. It's my time." This man kept pressing him, "Don't you know you're going to die?" Nat Turner tilted his head, looked at the fool and said, "Didn't Christ die?" He went on to his death a great black revolutionary.[15]

Now you've got time to worry about a mixed-up Europeans called Karl something-or-other? He never had any thought of you. He never gave you any thought of any consequence except the fact that you should be brought under the domination of European rule. You've got time to tell me what Lenin said but you can't tell me what David Walker said? You can't tell me what Henri Christophe or Toussaint L'Ouverture said?[16]

You never read Toussaint L'Ouverture's great letter to the Republicans of France? This is when he told the working class of France that they're doing you in too. "Napoleon wants to reconquer Haiti and bring the working class under control. But he wants to reconquer France and bring you under control, also."

You may have read a little of Karl Marx, maybe ten pages, maybe fifteen. Yet you will attack me, even threaten my life, on what Karl Marx said. But do you know what Du Bois said? Have you read *The Souls of Black Folk*? Have you read *The Gift of Black Folk*? Have you read his great master piece *Black Reconstruction*? Have you studied the historiography written in *Black Reconstruction*?[17]

No book written about the period was better structured or better researched than Du Bois' *Black Reconstruction*. You'll tell me about the rebuilding of Russia, which is alright. It's very interesting if you know that, but it's not relevant to you. Can you tell me how the partial freedom of black people challenged an entire society?[18]

Have you read Martin Delany's *The Condition, Elevation, Emigration and Destiny of Colored People of the United States*? Have you read that great preacher, Henry Highland Garnet? He said, "My moto is resistance, resistance, resistance." Did you hear Frederick Douglass when somebody asked him, "What are we going to do, Mr. Douglass, after you are gone?" Douglass said, "Agitate, agitate, agitate." You've got time for Karl something-or-other and you haven't heard of Frederick Douglass?[19]

I'm saying that when I look and listen again to the voices of my fathers, I look again at those great men and women who have gone on before me. They taught me through their literature, even if they didn't teach me through their life.

I remember the great poet, Georgia Douglass Johnson whose voting residence was New York City. Every time it was time to vote, Georgia Douglass Johnson would come from Washington, D.C. to New York City and vote. She was in her eighties and she would say, "I have to come in, cast my vote, and see my boys." There was Langston Hughes, myself, and a few other writers that she admired. She came to dine, scold us, and tell us what to do. Then she would return to Washington. We would say, "Miss Johnson, we'll send a car for you. We'll come down and meet you."

She said, "That's all right, boys. You've got your energy. You've got to use it to try to improve the lot of our people. Mama (referring to herself) is singing her September Song. But if you never see me again, remember I have used up my energy and I have used it well." And she did.

Now, in context with energy we need to ask ourselves, with all of the people in the world: Why did they enslave us and by-pass so many people? What do you have that they wanted so much? What do you have right now that the world wants? Energy. But you are not using that energy in your behalf. You have spent too much energy indulging in the degenerate forms of a dying people. We have not spent enough energy reviving ourselves, our own customs and our own culture.

When we deal with energy, we will deal with ourselves. Once we deal with the energy, we must deal with our great riches. If we had all the things that belong to us, not only would we be the riches people on the face of the earth, we would also be the most diverse and the most powerful. We would have all of the Caribbean. Population-wise we would have Brazil, several nations in South America, all of Africa (including the part which somebody says belongs to the Arabs). All that gold and manganese in South Africa, forty percent of all the known oil in the world. We would have rivers that have the greatest hydroelectric potential of any rivers in the world, right there in Africa.[20]

The rivers flow so naturally that many times you don't even have to build a dam. They flow so naturally that you can extract the electricity right out of the river. Africa could be the most electrified continent in the world, because the potential to produce electricity is higher in Africa than any other place in the whole world. We are neglecting that potential. We're eating wrong. We're dancing wrong. We're playing wrong. We're hanging out with the wrong people. We've got the wrong ideas. We've lost some confidence in doing for ourselves what we're asking other people to do for us.

If I must mention a very current event ... that retarded idiot called Wagner (Robert F. Wagner, Jr.). He is the newly elected president of the Board of Election. The vote is in. This man might read his name (if you put it in big letters). He is a school dropout. Now, there's nothing wrong with being a school dropout, because I am one. But I went on to educate myself out of school.

Thomas Minter, having been a superintendent of schools in three different cities, had every educational qualification. He received one vote out of the seven. Qualification doesn't get it in a society where you have no control. If someone else has to decide the rules of your existence, you are a prisoner to the person who made the decision. If you are peaceful and give everybody in the world a guarantee that you are going to be peaceful and not hurt anybody, there's nothing you can be in this kind of world but a slave.[21]

Looking at our history in its true light you have to look at the Africans who came to this country and the minute they could master the iceman's language, they tried to reclaim their history. You have to look at the history that was already made and how an entire people were completely lost from history. This happened because another people wanted to propagate the concept that the world waited in darkness for them to bring the light.[22]

Brothers and sisters, I have finished the preliminary remarks. I will now start the lecture. I have said in my notes (which I do not need) that this subject was well chosen and very timely. All of us need to take a good look at ourselves in relationship to our history and our destiny. I've also said that the true history of any people is the true history of the individuals in that society. When you look at your personal true history, you're looking at the history that is part of the history of a whole people.

I have looked back at those intellects who made an attempt to restructure our history. Our great historian William Leo Hansberry has said that Africa is the world's richest continent. I have asked if Africa is the world's richest continent, why are there so many poor people in Africa? Who has got our riches? Who's controlling our riches?

Europe is a poor group of nations. How did they build the skyscrapers? How did they build the ships at sea? They built their society by stealing your energy and your resources. Once you deploy your own energy right here in Harlem, there won't be a boarded-up house in Harlem. There won't be any dirty streets. That's because your energy, intellectually and physically, is going to take care of this.

What we are dealing with when we deal with history is the deployment of energy. When those Europeans came out of their thawed out icebox the first time, the Romans when they took over Carthage and North Africa making North Africa the breadbasket of the Roman Empire, were searching for energy: food, people, resources, aldn. Without the energy of Africa, there would have been no Roman Empire. That second time, without the energy of Africa in the fifteenth and sixteenth centuries, there would have been no modern Western world. You wouldn't have a subway or a shoe. Europe does not give up enough energy for that kind of building.[23]

We can build skyscrapers stretching to the moon with our own resources, not that we need skyscrapers at all. Land is so plentiful in a continent like Africa that you don't have to build a building that high. It's just not necessary to conserve space that way. Dealing with the word "conservative" or "conserve," went back and read the words of Martin Kilson, the late George Schuyler, and some others who called themselves black conservatives. I wondered what is it that they had to conserve. I guess the slave is trying to conserve the rope that they're going to use to hang him.[24]

No African person in the condition that we are in has got any business being anything but a radical. Our contact with the West started in revolt and it must continue. We need to pay attention to great figures among us who tried to preserve our history.

We must look at the nineteenth century. We must look again at certain Europeans who made a valiant effort to preserve our history, to set it in its true light, while other Europeans were distorting it. By all means, read Gerald Massey. There is no place you can find the documentation, the momumental truth of the Africaness/blackness of Egypt better documented than in Gerald Massey.

Then we can go to the American Alvin Boyd Kuhn, especially in his book, *Who Is this King of Glory?* and *The Shadow of the Third Century*. *Who Is this King of Glory?* shows how the whole concept of the Christ was stolen from Africa. Then in *Shadow of the Third Century* he shows what the great African father of the Church, St. Augustine, thought of all this mishmash that the Europeans had cooked up at the Council of Nicea (325 A.D.). Augustine said, "It makes me laugh. It's ridiculous." Augustine went on to create the literature that became the basis of that religion.

I think the first thing that we need to do is to read our interpretation of the religion before the Europeans tampered with it, even before they gave it a name. Once we look at it, all the religions properly used are great. You can adhere to any one of them as long as you make it what you want it to be. Everything that touches your life must be an instrument of your liberation or it must be discarded.

We cannot travel with excess luggage. We cannot carry around things we do not need. We cannot be cute. We must come straight to the problem. The problem with the world of today, we solved that long ago. That is the problem of feeding, housing, schooling, and the problem of protection. We had that settled. We did not need anybody to come in and tell us that.

The Europeans all have documentation. They did not find one hungry or underfed person in all Africa. Africans had figured that out before they even saw a European. In spite of all the supposition to the point and all of the writing, there is not a European alive or dead who can prove they saw one so-called cannibal. That's another lie that they kept repeating until they began to believe it.

What we have to do is to begin to criticize these men. This does not make us less religious because we know that the Exodus is a Hebrew folktale. We are not less religious because we know that the Noah story not only didn't occur, but couldn't have occurred. We are not less religious because we have read Sir George James Frazer's *The Folklore of the Old Testament* and we have traced flood stories throughout all of the civilizations. Everybody has their flood story. And everybody has their Christ story. You are entitled to make one of your own because it relates to you.[25]

Years ago as a young writer I wrote a short story called "The Boy Who Painted Christ Black." It dealt with a boy who appointed Christ to resemble his father. The white superintendent of schools expelled the black principal for defending the child's right to paint God to resemble what is a deity in his life.[26]

The father, properly looked on, and the mother too are deities. They brought you here. Those two people got together and through that relationships you came into the world. They could have left you some place. They brought you there. They loved you. They changed your diaper. They scolded you. You didn't look to the heavens when you wanted food. You said, "Hey, Mama, I want some."[27]

The essential things in your life came from Mama. The essential things that kept Mama paying those bills and creating those miracles with the little amount of money was Papa. Put both of them together and you have deities. You have holy people who performed a miracle. They got together and brought a full human being into the world. That is the right of people to look at their mothers, fathers, and their families, to look at them as the givers of their spiritual and intellectual life.

This is why my old grandmother kept visiting me in the hospital and kept on visiting me when I went home. I kept wondering, "Grandma, are you ever going to stop wearing the black dress?" Grandma always had a black dress on, always had a cane, and always told me to keep faith in myself, run the race of life, and run it with faith.

When something tampers with your faith—I think something tampered with mine and I had to re-adjust it—when people I thought were friends of mine came down on me with a false charge; when it was brought up not one person of the group I trusted came to my defense . . . then I was wondering what it was all about.

The greatest thing I could have done—and had I done this I would not have had a stroke at all—I should have picked up my hat and coat and told those Brothers and Sisters, "You are confused. Go to hell. Goodby." When people are being ridiculous, sometimes the best thing to do is to put space between you and them.

In looking at Europeans who wrote favorably about Africans and got themselves in trouble for doing so, I was looking back at the works of Count Volney and his statement upon observing Ethiopia then in decline. He said:

> They are a people now forgotten who, while others were yet barbarians, created the elements of the arts and the sciences. A race of men, rejected from society because of their sable skin and frizzled hair, created the civil laws that now govern the Universe.[28]

This man had a streak of honesty and realized that he was in the presence of a people, though in decline, who created the laws that now govern the whole world, and he said so. If he said so and you can't go back to some of the wisdom of our own people to free yourselves, you have confusion. If you don't know Karl Marx from Groucho Marx, you are confused.

We need to look at those three great Germans who went to Africa in the 1800's. First, Heinrich Barth, who could read Arabic and understand some African languages. When making an assessment of that Songhai Empire and the career of Askia he Great, the last of the great rulers of state that we had in Africa before the decline, Barth called him one of the great civil administrators of all time.[29]

Then we go back again to a German, Arnold Hermann Ludwig Heeren, who wrote (1837) the masterwork on the trade, the intercourse between the Egyptians, the Ethiopians, and the Carthanginians. When we go back and look at what other people saw in us and the great potential we had in us, we wonder why we have failed to see our history in its true light by seeing the same potential in ourselves.

What we have to do its to be totally honest with ourselves and we must acknowledge that, in the great propaganda war, we lost faith in ourselves. Once we restore faith in ourselves, we will draw strength from our own history instead of looking at the history of our slavemasters. What we need to do is to look at a new frame of reference. We must look at the names and as our remarkably young historian Lerone Bennett has said, "We have been named. We shall be namers." We must reach the point of rejecting what other people say of us by telling them who they are.

We must tell those fools who came out of Europe that there is no such thing as a race anyway, least of all there's no such thing as a White race. If I see a human being the color of a sheet of paper, I will give it up and run like hell because I would have seen a ghost.[30]

People are mixed up in their naming of people but more mixed up in their naming of us. We are confused in accepting these bogus names. Wherever we are on the face of this earth, we are an African people. The failure of modern Africa and her leadership is that not a single head of state had the nerve to build a truly African state as opposed to a pseudo mishmash Western state.

Once you build a truly African state and draw on the strength of African philosophy, you are going to have the role model of what the world of tomorrow still must be. Do not think that you will be depriving yourself of modernism. You will not be depriving yourself of running water. The great scholars of Timbuctoo during its height told their students, "Believe in God and science." God and science was one and the same thing. They had never heard a European say God is science and science is God. Philosophy is sacred.[31]

In these societies, which some fools call primitive, certain men were told to sit down and think. "I'll bring you your sandals. I'll bring you your bread. Your job is to do one thing: to think." Then when the people have confusion, they will ask, "Oh, thinker, how do we come out of this confusion?"

We have not produced a thinker that will bring us out of confusion. We have produced a lot of money-changers, male prostitutes for the establishment. They know how to get to the bank and deposit their thirty pieces of silver, but they don't know how to tell you how to revolutionize the community ... even just starting with just the revolution of a boarded-up house. If I tell you how Songhai was ruled by a single man and if you can't run a candy store in Harlem, you're missing my point. That's because the role of history is to tell you what you have been, what you are, and what you still must be.

Now, I will try to conclude a lecture that I have barely started. The subject is bigger than the hour. I have been looking at African History in its true light, or searching for it, for most of my life. When as a Baptist Sunday school teacher (barely twelve) I saw all of those white characters in the bible, when I looked in the Bible and saw Moses (an African) turning white and saw Zipporah (an Ethiopian) turning white, I went to the pastor and asked, "Why are these people white when the contintent is supposed to be black?" He said, "Hush up, boy. You cannot doubt God's word." I did not know then that it wasn't God's word at all. It was the word of a Baptist Sunday School publisher owned by Whites in Nashville, Tennessee.[32]

I was then searching for African History in its true light as a teacher, as a researcher, and as a student under the great master teachers like Willlis Huggins, William Leo Hansberry, Arthur Schomburg, Charles C. Siefert, and others. I did not feel hesitant about sitting at their feet and asking these great masters to tell me what history is all about.[33]

Therefore, in preparing these notes, I have tried to point to some of the main currents in our history that have brought us to where we are and what we will have to do in order to get out of the predicament that we are in. I have looked at the works of the great Richard B. Moore who died in Barbados a few years ago. I've looked at his statement that no one would have gone to so much trouble to cover up the history of a people who had no history. If they had no history, you could just let it be. However, if you have history that they want to cover up, it takes an effort.

I have, as a teacher and a researcher, looked at African people within the mail currents of the history of the world. At every single time that Europe came out, it came out to rob you of the energy they needed to survive. They're doing it in South Africa right now.

I've told some of these Africans who advocate a multiracial government that you are dreaming and playing the fool. Those who say that we will share the government with the Whites are also playing the fool. I will not share any part of my house with the thief who came into my house against my will. If I share the part of the earth of my house with him—in my home, my country—I pay him the compliment of a grave and I will plant flowers over his head. You show me an example where any European ever shared power with a non-European and I'll consider your offer. If he won't share power with you in his country what makes you think you've got to share power with them in your country?

What we have to do is to create and begin to use the term "an African state." A state where all men can walk in dignity and peace, so long as they understand this is an African state.

African people are in charge and will stay in charge. We're not so stupid that we would form an African branch of the Ku Klux Klan. We don't need this nonsense. However, we will protect ourselves and if you bring one to us, we will wash them away.

We need to look at the basis of our humanity as a people and look at those great things that have gone on before us. In looking at those things we need to draw the proper precedents from history. We need to learn what history is supposed to do for us. What we also need to do is to plant the seed into this generation what will make the generations still to come.[34]

What you might call a failure of the Civil Rights Movement was the failure to establish a continuity between the fight that went on before, the fight that's going on now, and the fight that still must go on. If some of these youth knew what old Nat Turner did, they would have known what to do in Birmingham against Bull Conner. They did not know what Nat Turner did. They did not know what Denmark Vesey did. They did not know what Toussaint L'Ouverture did. And they did not know what Christophe learned from Toussaint L'Ouverture.

If Toussaint were alive today, he would be a petit bourgeois, partly conservative. He held up that revolution so some French who had partly befriended him could escape. In a revolution you've got no friends and you've got no relatives. You've got the people on your side and the ones not on your side. If blood don't see fit to come on your side, then shame on blood. That's what it means to be in a revolution.

We have to look at history as a guideline of our being. I would like to conclude by paraphrasing Saunders Redding's speech on the African writer and his roots when he said that a writer's relationship to his roots relates to his totality. He said, in effect, "A people's relationship to their roots is the sum total of all their creative effort. To relate to your roots, meaning your history, is to teach how to be a better instrument in dealing with other people." Finally, he said, "A people's relationship to their history is the same as the relationship of a child to its mother."[35]

Chapter Three

The Contribution of Nile Valley Civilization to World Civilization

Cleveland, Ohio
July 17, 1992

I have a short time to deliver a long message. Otherwise, I'll reminisce about the time as a teenager when I came through Cleveland and was eighteen years old. I was on my way to Chicago. Chicago turned me down and I ended up in New York. However, I've got to get to work. I'll go straight to the subject.

Why are we talking about Egypt out of context with the rest of Africa? Why do you dare talk about my left hand out of context with my right hand, as though both of them are not a part of my body? When we talk about Egypt, let's make one thing clear: you are talking about Africa.

On this point I give no ground. I do not yield one inch of Africa as a part of the Middle East. I reject the very words "middle east" as the creation of the British Colonial Office. There is no such thing as the Middle East. There is Western Asia, however middle of where, middle of what?[1]

Now, I'm going to talk about the contribution of Nile Valley civilization to world civilization. I have spoken on this subject many times over the years. I am no longer argumentative about the subject. The evidence of the Africanness of Nile Valley civilization, the evidence of Egypt being solely and purely African is so clear. The argument is an offense to my intelligence and yours.

I will proceed with the assumption that you know what I am talking about. When I say Egypt, I'm talking about a country in Africa that the Greeks called Aegyptus and that the Africans never called Egypt. I'm talking about Nile Valley civilization and I'm talking about a river that stretches four thousand miles into the body of Africa. It related to all of the people along that river valley. Egypt was not a singular civilization but a composite civilization which was composed of all of the cultures and ethnic elements of that entire valley. Egypt was not a civilization in itself, but a culmination of a number of civilizations, all of them originally coming from the south.

In their own literature, *The Papyrus of Henefer*, they said, "we came from the foothills of the Mountains of the Moon where the Great God, Hapi dwells." Hapi was one of the early gods of Nile Valley civilization. Tranlated, 'Mountains of the Moon' means Kilimanjaro. The Nile Valley is a contradiction as a river. It starts in the south and flows to the north. Most rivers of the world start in the north and flow to the south. Since it starts in the south and flows to the north, what you think is the first cataract is really the sixth cataract. You are moving into Egypt down the Nile Valley. The foreigners got it exactly backwards because they were "beholden" to Europe, and Europe gets a whole lot of things backwards.

Hear me well, the main contribution of Nile Valley civiliza-tion to world civilization is the concept of civilization itself. Nile Valley civilization contributed organized societies, social order, the concept of coming together, the concept of the village uniting with other villages, creating the cities, the concept of cities uniting with other cities creating a state, and the concept of other areas (states) uniting with other areas creating a concept that would later be called diplomacy.

Nile Valley civilization contributed the idea of getting together, one to the other, creating a concept of human relationships and survival. In early agriculture we created something after the radical nature of the river calmed down and stopped overflowing irregularly and began to overflow at a specific time. We knew when to get out of the way of the river and when to come back and plant in the rich earth on its banks. They created the world's first massive agriculture.

By creating the world's first massive agriculture, they could develop a technical class and a laboring class which could be taken care of. People down this valley would gravitate toward the end of the river and bring their technical skills, goods, and services. Therefore, they made the river the world's first cultural highway.

To build a basic civilization, you've got to have enough resources food and the ability to pay craftsmen and technicians) to sustain yourself. When you've got enough and some left over, you build an intellectual civilization that explains and preserves the original civilization. Since they had time to sit some men down and let them think for a living, they created literature. Out of this literature came a spirituality. Out of this spirituality came all of the elements that went into the making of the three major religions. Spirituality is real. Organized religion is a formation of man.

Nearly everything that is a formation of man has some defect. If you create a formation out of someone else's spirituality which you do not understand and say, "I am a chosen people," you are saying someone else is not chosen, therefore making God ungodly. If you create from that spirituality—the elements created—and say, "I have the true faith," you are saying other people's faith must be false. If you create another religion which says that my religion gives me the right to enslave you because you are an infidel, you are making God an accessory to murder.

The misunderstanding of the spirituality extracted from Africa and the opportunistic remolding of it into something which rationalizes someone's domination over another people has made all organized religions, to some degree, atheistic because they deny by their actions that God is love and that God is kind and merciful.

Now let's get to the bottom of it, because while Nile Valley Civilization made a major contribution, and that original contribution came from the south, there were other contributions of other river valleys that we do not have the time to discuss, principally the Niger, the Congo, the Limpopo, the Zambezi, and the Volta. Most great civilizations start near rivers.[2]

One thing that is so inconceivable to you, because of the success of massive propaganda, is that over half of human history was over before anyone knew that the European was in the world. Because of massive propaganda, assumptions, and a change which occurred in the fifteenth and sixteenth centuries (the juncture of our enslavement and the beginning of European world dominance), they had to make people believe that the world waited in darkness for them to bring the light. According to them, everything good came form them. Yet they put out morelights than they ever lit. They destroyed more civilizations than they ever created. We need to understand that fact in order to put history in proper focus.[3]

When you look at the chronology of history you will know there was no European in ancient times. When the ancient world emerged there was no Europe. Europe emerged at the end of the ancient world, at the beginning of the modern world. It took advantage of the fall of the ancient world. It copied from ancient peoples and it put its name on things it did not develop. It was like a faker, a liar, and a murderer who discovered absolutely nothing ... he is being celebrated now five hundred years after the mass murder he set in motion. Such genocide would make Hitler look like a Sunday school boy.[4]

What I'm trying to get at is that this first European view of Africa was somewhat strange, but a compliment. When we first meet the African image in the *Iliad* and the *Odyssey* ien Greek mythology, it is complimentary. It's strange and untrue, but it's complimentary. People who are ten feet tall with one eye in the middle of their head. That's strange, but it's not an absolute insult. The Greeks thought that they (the Egyptians) were the favorites of the gods. Even Prophet Mohamet called them "the righteous people." He told his followers, "Go to Ethiopia, go to that righteous land where no one is wrong." This was as late as the seventeenth century A.D.

How then did we get a reputation as a people who needed to be led into the light by a "civilized" people who thought we were primitive? How did we become primitive when we knew long before they wore shoes and lived in a house that had a window. We had created an honorable way of life and had every element that went into the making of Socialism and Christianity? We had no word for jail because nobody had ever gone to one. There was no world for orphanage because no one had ever thrown away any children. There were no old people's homes because nobody threw away grandma and grandpa.

The sustaining ideology that went to awaken Mediterranean Europe (I'm using the term "Mediterranean Europe" because there was no Europe at the time. I can make a better case for Greece and Rome not being a part of Europe than you can make for Egypt not being a part of Africa) came from outside of Europe.

During the period of Greece and Rome, politically there was no functioning Europe. During the period of Egypt there was not only a fully functioning Africa, but Egypt had relationships with the rest of Africa in trade.

Just for fun, let's say the Egyptians were white. Now if they associated with Africans for 5,000 years and their labor supply, priests, and a lot of their technicians came from the South, after 5,000 years would they still be white? Men don't go 5,000 miles away, all the way back home, to satisfy their biological urges.

Let's play around with another idea. Let's say that the Europeans built the pyramids. The pyramids were built when the Ice Ages were thawing out in Europe. How would Europeans come from under the ice, come all the way to Africa, build the pyramids, go all the way back to Europe, and stay there 2,000 years before they made a shoe or a house with a window? Then failing to do that, they don't even begin to produce a book until about 1,200 B.C. which is a piece of folklore by somebody named Homer. We don't know whether Homer is a man or a woman.[5]

The literature of the Nile Valley was already in tact. *The Book of Coming Forth by Night and Day* was already in tact, out of which others would copy a lot of the elements that would go into the Bible. Out of which others would copy the basis of the Ten Commandments from the Forty Two Confessions. You should never use the word "negative" in relation to those confessions, that's a European interpretation. They weren't negative at all. These were admissions of faith and purity.[6]

You would stand before your master teacher and say, "I have not done this." Not, "thou shalt not," but "I have not." I have not violated my neighbor's wife. I have not taken my neighbor's property. I have not done this. If you had not done all of those things, then you were qualified for something. The European changed the language around to "thou shalt not." The Africans originally did not say "Thou shalt not." They said, "I have not."

The Europeans would extract from Nile Valley literature the spirituality and elements that would go into making the world's three major religions. This is an argument for most Blacks who are Moslems, but most Blacks who are Moslems are not true Moslems, they are Arabists. "Islam is the Black man's true religion." Okay, I agree with you. Every organized religion is the black man's true religion because every element that went into the making of it came out of Africa.

Now this great meeting in history extracted from Nile Valley civilization the means of other civilizations and complemented civilizations like the Tigris and the Euphrates, and the early civilizations of the Greeks (before they were called Greeks). The Greeks at this point were intellectual dumb bunnies, but that's another subject. All this was extracted from Western Asia and North Africa, coming by the way of Nile Valley civilization. This river would be the world's greatest cultural highway.

In order to get these things straight, there's certain terminology in history you'll have to throw into the ashcan. You have to stop using the term "Negro Africa." There's no such thing as a "Negro" area. There's no such thing as people called Negro. We'll have to stop using the term "Black Africa" because it presupposes that there is a legitimate "White Africa."

Be careful about the term "Arab Africa." There are Arabs who live in Africa, but there is no part of Africa that rightfully belongs to them. Whether you like it or not, they too are invaders. Everybody in Africa who cannot be referred to as an Africa is either an invader or the descendants of invaders ... be clear on that point. Once you are clear on that point, and you are clear that Africa is your home and your house in the world, you don't get into silly arguments about "sharing."

I don't share my house. I don't share my wife. I will share Africa the same way you are willing to share Europe with me. This is why we can't straighten out the situation in South Africa. If you have a house with six rooms and you only need four and you catch a thief in one of the rooms, you do not negotiate with the thief for one room. If you catch him, you negotiate with the undertaker to take the dead thief away.[8]

Now I feel the Baptist preacher in me and this is the time when I should be winding up. What I want to let you know is that most Whites who pretend that they don't know the real truth about Egypt and the real truth about Egypt's connection with the rest of Africa, especially Ethiopia and the Sudan have known the truth all along. In fact it was the radical literature of these Whites which set the radical Blacks in motion.

They have to pretend to you that they had not read these masterpieces written by the Whites on the same subject. They never quote Gerald Massey and his six volume work, *Egypt, Light of the World*; his two volume work, *Signs and Symbols of Primordial Man* or his great American disciple Alvin Boyd Kuhn and his work entitled *Who Is This King of Glory?* The introduction to the book tells you how the Hebrews copied so much of the text that went into the Bible which came from the literature of Nile Valley civilization.

When I use the word "Hebrew" I might be confusing you and myself because I know better. I know that when these Western Asians entered Africa they were not Hebrew, but they were Hebrew when they left. When they entered Africa they had no clear religion, no clear language, and no clear culture; they had all three when they left. So who are we talking about? We are talking about a people who effected a wedding between their culture in Western Asia and the culture they encountered in Africa, and who belonged to the Hebrew faith.[9]

I'm separating the religion and the faith from the people. I am doing something most of us don't do; we just read words. We don't look behind the words and look at the visitors, the invaders of Africa. We don't look at the monumental literature explaining Africa by Europeans and then go to the monumental literature explaining Africa by Africans. There were three Germans: Hereen (a six-volume work; especially his fourth volume, *A History of the Commercial Intercourse between the Egyptians, the Ethiopians, and the Carthaginians*), the second German Heinrich Barth wrote *Travels and Discoveries in North and Central Africa* (three volumes; *The Temple Edition*, five volumes), and the third German, Leo Grobenius, wrote a five-volume *History of African Civilization.* It was condensed into two volumes called *The Voice of Africa*.[10]

Then to the English. There was William Flinders-Petrie and Gerald Massey. Massey worked forty years in the field. He was an agnostic; he wasn't even an Africanist. He wasn't even an African lover. He said, "I will prove that all European religions were taken from outside of Europe." He kept tracing them back to Africa. He wrote a small pamphlet called *The Historical Jesus and the Cystic Christ*. Also there was the work done by the French, namely Gaston Maspero and Maurice Delafosse.[11]

There's no mystery about Egypt and no mystery about Nile Valley contribution, all of this is documented. If you don't want to read the Black documents, then read the white ones. Read Count Volney's work, *The Ruins of Empire*. There was another Frenchman, De Lepsis, who did an assessment of the monumental ruins. Read Herodotus, the first eye-witness account; the Roman historians on Africa, Pliny the Elder and Pliny the Younger. Read what Herodotus said about the complexion of the Egyptians and Ethiopians being the same.[12]

By 450 B.C. Egypt had been invaded by one army after another from Western Asia. They had been bastardized and "mulattoized" and everything else by then, and yet they were still basically a black people as late as 450 B.C. Then what did happen to that vast black population in North Africa? Every invader hit that population from the North, driving them further to the south and driving some out of Africa altogether. If you want to find their descendants, you find them right within the body of Africa.[13]

After the initial first invasion of Northeast Africa (1675 B.C.), 1,000 years later than the Assyrian (now Syria) invasions came in 666 B.C., came the Iranians (then calling themselves Persians) in 550 B.C. They were so brutal that Africans cried out, "Oh, God, if you cannot send me a liberator, then bring us a conqueror who will show mercy." When the young conqueror, Alexander of Macedonia, knocked on the door—he didn't have to knock very hard. To Alexander's everlasting credit, he did show mercy. When he beheld the greatness of the Africa of his day, almost a thousand years on the scene, he wrote home, "This is the home of Zeus and Apollo. This is where the Greek Gods started."

The Romans wanted to control the Mediterranean and finally defeated Hannibal and took over North Africa. This is a subject which requires some explantation because the Roman Empire rose in Africa and it fell in Africa. There were more African Christians killed in the Roman amphitheaters in North Africa than Christians in the arena in Rome. The African persecution side of the Christian story has not been told.[14]

The murder of the African woman teacher/catechist, Hypatia, was at the hands of the Romans. Finally the Romans stopped killing Christians and became Christians. Their mismanagement of Christianity was so terrible because it didn't fit their character then and it doesn't fit it now. Early in the 7th century A.D., a camel boy began to grumble and ask for reform. Failing to get reform, he asked for a new religion, that new religion was Islam.[15]

The Africans thought that by opening the door to the Arabs, they could get the Romans off their backs. They were right. They got the Romans off their backs and the Arabs replaced the Romans on their backs. The Africans had merely exchanged conquerors. Islam did some good things and some bad things. There was a strange equality in Islamic thugism. They permitted the Africans to join them in beating other non-Islamic people into submission. The Africans came with their military armies. They were almost the sole military arm in the initial conquest of Spain. This is something that needs to be told, because when the Arabs and the Europeans tell the story they leave out the Africans.

This story is well told by John G. Jackson, one of our senior historians, in his *Introduction to African Civilization* in the chapter called "Africa and the Civilizing of Europe." Also, Stanley Lane-Poole (an Englishman) did an excellent job with his work, *The Moors in Spain.*[16]

I've only gone part of the way and I can repeat the beginning. What Nile Valley civilization contributed to human civilization are those elements that collectively went into the making of civilization itself.[17]

We, as a people, are now at another crossroad in history. We've lived through a 500-year holocaust that is not completely over. Fate has not spared us for any idle purpose. When we look throughout the world there are Africans in Asia, the Pacific Islands, South America, the Caribbean Islands, the United States, and in Africa itself. In spite of the AIDS created to destroy us, there are one billion of us on the face of this earth.[18]

Maybe we have a lesson to teach the world about a new humanity. We are the only people who can claim what rightfully belongs to us without encroaching on anything that belongs to other people. Maybe we are in a position to ask for a new beginning. Maybe we can ask for a revolution that will start humankind over again. I'm saying seek a pattern to assist you by finding a mirror and see who's staring back at you. If you have some doubts you might say you're going to start your revolution tomorrow or the next day, but all serious revoutuionists once they start understanding the nature of and the need for social change, they will say in essence, "Here I am, Lord, send me. I will start my revolution today."

Chapter Four

Pan-Africanism in Transition:
Looking Toward the Twenty-First Century

I have referred to Pan-Africanism as an evolving idea in the African world. Pan-Africanism is often misunderstood because there is no acceptable operational definition of Pan-Africanism that prevails throughout the whole of the African world. Formal Pan-Africanism is the creation of Caribbean intellects. I think it reached its greatest acceptance in the United States among Black Americans during the period of Marcus Garvey, 1916-1927. I think the unannounced mission of Pan-Africanism is to facilitate and bring about the ingathering of African people throughout the world and to restore what slavery and colonialism took away.

This is a critical time and this is time for a curious debate among us—a debate at the threshold of liberation that has gone on too long. We, as a people, figuratively speaking, may have rehearsed for a hundred years for a show which we are afraid to put on the road. We have to end the rehearsal and put the show on the road, warts and all.

My notes for tonight are called "Pan-Africanism in Transition: Looking Toward the Twenty-First Century." To look toward the twenty-first century, I must look backwards and forward at the same time. I must first look back at the fifteenth century. At the five-hundred-year span of time, the age of menticide, and explain the colonization of our mind that has brought us to the sad state where we can get close to liberation, close enough to touch it and taste it and then turn around and move in the other direction. When you keep a people out of power so long, they long desperately for power. And when they get close to power, they panic.

Willis N. Huggins, of the old Harlem History Club, told me the story. I didn't believe it then and never thought I would be watching it in action fifty years later. He said, "John, we, as a people, will have no difficulty getting to the door of the promised land. We will get to the door of the promised land, and we will bunch up and start an argument about whether we cross the threshold with our left foot or our right." This is because slavery is an adjustment. The aftermath of chattel slavery is an adjustment to a new kind of slavery. As long as you are dependent on other people solely for your jobs, your house, the cleaning of your streets, the education of your children, the image you see on television, or the image of God in your Church, you can cut it any way you want to, you are a slave.

What I'm talking about is a concept called Pan-Africanism which has as its mission the freedom of our mind from dependency on others so that we can be free to behave again as a nation of people free of dependency on other people, free of dependency on other people's images, free of dependency on other people's interpretation of God.

When the Europeans began to colonize and enslave the world in the fifteenth and sixteenth centuries, they not only would colonize the world geographically, they would colonize information about the world. Then they would colonize images. The most disastrous aspect of colonization which you are the most reluctant to release from your mind is their colonization of the image of God.[1]

After these years of colonization, you dare not address

God in a language of your creation. You dare not imagine him through your own imagination. You worship a picture painted by Michelangelo fourteen hundred years after Christ died. You have never challenged Michelangelo. And if I told you there was a possibility that Christ could have been black, I'd have a hard time getting out of the room with my life. Yet, Christ was born in that part of the world that is predominantly non-European. One should never get into an argument about his color—Black, white, or otherwise—anyway. All you have to do is ask whether he was a Roman. No, he was not a Roman. Was he A Greek? No, he wasn't a Greek. So, whatever he was, he was one of those "other" people, and all of those "other" people were not white. You can argue about his shade, but I don't have time for that. I only want to establish the fact that there was no way possible for him to be a white European. Then once I establish that, I let you argue about the shade.

Because we do not read enough, we worship a religion, spend a fortune on it, and we do not understand the re-creation of this *religion* at the Council of Nicea when they made it European, killed all the blackness, took out the Black Madonnas and the Black images. It's been White ever since. They even threw out the Black angels.[2]

Now this is digression, but it makes the point. I'm going to Pan-Africanism. Don't think I've forgotten the subject, now. Years ago, I grew up in Alabama with a burning love for my great grandmother who is still a deity in my life. I am very fortunate in my attitude toward people and the warmth and gentleness of my personality, because the three deities that lived and walked on this earth who still influence my life (though they've been dead over fifty years) were always my mother, my great grandmother, and my fifth grade teacher.

Under the influence of my great grandmother, reading the Bible to me and teaching me how to pronounce words like Deuteronomy, I wanted to teach Sunday school. To teach

Sunday school, I had to learn how to read. So I learned to read very early for a very selfish reason; I wanted to teach the junior class in Sunday school. Finally, I made it long before I was ten.

There I was, up there teaching the little Sunday school lessons sent down from a white Baptist publishing company in Tennessee. All the angels were white. Moses was white. Moses goes down to Ethiopia to marry Zipporah, and Zipporah gets white. Moses would go to the land of Kush (present-day Sudan), and the people in the Sudan get white. You could go to the Sudan right now and you would see the most beautiful velvety black people. They have a sheen. I've never seen such beautiful blackness in my life. Smooth, velvety blackness. People going to the land of Puanit, or Punt, present-day Somalia they were black then, they're black now. They were black then. But in the Bible story, they got white.

I go to great grandma, she says, "This is God's book." I say, "Grandma, how did we get left out of God's book?" "Shut up, boy." This is somebody I love now, so I'm not going to argue with her. But I never stopped until I found some answers. I kept wondering why the angels bothered me so. If God was love, with all the people in the world, he couldn't sneak in one little brown angel? One little black angel?

This set me out looking at history in general and when early in New York I heard (for the first time) the word Pan-Africanism, I began to look it up and read essays about it. I found there was nothing especially new about Pan-Africanism. The same as we had Christianity before people gave it a name, we had Pan-Africanism before people gave it a name. And we had Africancentricity before people put a name on it and called it Afrocentricity, which is an error, because there is no "fro" in Africa. People are putting "new" coats on "old" things, formulizing them and dogmatizing them and giving you the illusion that they are giving you something new. They are rehashing old African ceremonies and telling you that they are giving you a substitute for Christmas, when you could have created the same thing yourself had you taken time to think about it.

I'm not saying don't celebrate Kwanzaa. I think it's a good idea. That's not my argument. My argument is not against it. My argument is against the fake claims made around it and all of the phonies who are palming off the concept that they invented it, when it was here all along. All they did was formalize it, dogmatize it, and give it a name.

I define Pan-Africanism as any effort on the part of African people to reclaim any portion of Africa that has been taken away, mutilated, misunderstood, or misinterpreted by a non-African to the detriment of Africa. Therefore, my definition goes beyond the word, "Pan," which means "all." When I look back at the historical role and the historical manifestations of Pan-Africanism, I deal with the first organized society in the Nile Valley, when the people of the South and the people of the North (the Upper and the Lower Nile) came together to roam a country now known to the world as Egypt. They picked a family to rule and called the family a dynasty. When that family had given to the state the best of its creative energy, they switched to another family. It was the beginning of dynasties, the beginning of royalty, the beginning of high responsibility in the state. The unification of the Upper Nile and the Lower Nile was an act of Pan-Africanism, putting a portion of Africa together for the whole of Africa to be together.

When the people of East Africa, along the coast, began to develop city-states and began to bring these states together in a trading network which the Arabs called the balad-as-Sudan (or the Land of the Blacks), you have an East African form of Pan-Africanism. Now you've got a Nile Valley form of pan-Africanism. You have Africans moving together around the Nile River. Later on, with the weakening of the states of the Nile, you have the beginning of great states on the Niger. From Ghana, Mali, and Songhai, you have the development of great states in

Inner Africa. When these states functioned well together and warded off all foreigners, you had another form of Pan-Africanism existing within Africa itself.[3]

This, of course, would continue for a thousand years. Nations, like people, sometimes get tired and careless. You can say it began to fall after a thousand years. But the Roman Empire at its best, in fact lasted less than seven hundred years. The glories of the Roman empire have been well promoted. However, there were African states that lasted twice as long as that which you don't even know about. Once you know about them then, "They were better. They did this. They did that." The Romans fell for reasons the Africans didn't fall for.

No African state ever fell because there was mass degeneracy. The Romans, overdressed, smug, and sick of war, hired foreigners to do their fighting. They started neglecting schools. They hired foreigners to take over their education. Mass homosexuality—women got on their nerves—foreigners took over the responsibility of pleasing their women. So, if a present-day Italian tells you that he is a descendant of an Ancient Roman, do not laugh directly in his face. Have good manners, cup your hand and laugh to one side. He is the bastard child of a bastard child. One of our distant relatives, over there "passing." This is why they're so brutal on us, because we know their "name" and their "game." All these Mediterranean mulattoes getting over at our expense, that includes all the Spaniards who were once a part of us. Once they boasted about it. Let's get back to Pan-Africanism, because that's another lecture over there.[4]

With the rise of Islam, you have a form of religious gangster Pan-Africanism. I know I'm in trouble, but that's my job. The Arabs, who swept out of the East and conquered North Africa, were religious gangsters then and they're religious gangsters now. In spite of that little drama (called the Persian War) in the sand where nobody can win, that's another situation.

The Africans who had grown so sick of Roman rulers who had taken over Christianity and had mutilated it to the point where Christianity became revolting, these Africans welcomed the Arabs because they thought the Arabs would get the Romans off their backs. The Arabs did get the Romans off their backs and replaced the Romans on their backs, where they still are.

The main point here is when Islam spread into Inner West Africa—because Africans are puritans. We are true believers. We out-Pope the Pope and we out-Mahomet Mahomet. The Africans who had been converted by the Arabs went to North Africa and told those Arabs, "You are not properly observing the faith." Finally, Gebel Tarik moved over and conquered Spain. The Arab's control over Spain did not take place until fifty years later. The books on the subject used to be hard to find. They are starting to be re-published in paperback now. Read Stanley Lane-Poole's work, *The Story of the Moors in Spain*. Read John G. Jackson's introduction to that book. If you have John Jackson's book, *Introduction to African Civilization*, read his chapter, "The Africans and the Civilizing of Europe." If you're fortunate enough to have Eleanor Hoffman's book, *Realm of the Evening Star: Morocco and the Land of the Moors*, read the chapter on the rape of Timbuctoo. It tells how the Arabs from the North, who were Moslems, destroyed Timbuctoo in the land of the Black Moslems. You will lose your romance with the religion, because that religion, anytime it suited itself to do so, has never hesitated in turning on Africans.[5]

One thing that we fail to understand is that we have no friends in this world and we owe the world nothing but a whipping. This is because everybody, who has not already turned on us, has proved that they would do it anytime it was to their convenience economically. We number a billion people on the face of this earth. Maybe if we look into a mirror and start making friends with ourselves, maybe we wouldn't need any other friends.

Now, with the emergence of Europe in the 1400's, the making of the slave trade, the breaking-up of the African family structure, the scattering of the Africans away from home, the scattering of the Africans to the Caribbean islands, we began to manifest forms of patriotism three hundred years before H. Sylvester Williams called a conference on Pan-Africanism in 1900 in London. In the Caribbean islands, revolt after revolt, culminating in the Haitian Revolt, which brought to power the first nation of former slaves in history. There was the Berbice Revolt in Guyana and the Maroon Revolts in Jamaica. There were other revolts in Jamaica not related to the Maroons but very successful revolts. They were led by great leaders and, unfortunately, they are forgotten by history: Mansong, Tacky, Gordon's Revolt.[6]

Jamaicans began to understand that their freedom (emancipation) was a fake. So when Caribbean people say that, "Our emancipation came thirty years before your emancipation . . ." C'mon. Your fakery came thirty years before our fakery, because right now we're still not free. Neither one of us needs to boast and neither one of us needs to apologize. But we need to realize our position and develop a means of putting us back together to cure the fragmentation of slavery and colonialism. The formal literature, the dogma and the basic plan of Pan-Africanism would start in the Caribbean islands with the mentality of the Caribbean people who, then, had more intellectual freedom than the Blacks in the United States.[7]

However, after the first conference, the lot would fall to W.E.B. Du Bois who would carry it from the first conference through the fourth conference. At the fifth conference, all three elements would come together in Manchester, England and form a Pan-African Congress which would lay the basis for the future independence of African states. All of this is well defined in George Padmore's little work, *Pan-Africanism, or Commu-*

nism? and again in C.L.R. James' little work *A History of Pan African Revolt.* Nobody is hiding the literature from you. Some of you will debate forever about a subject and wouldn't entertain opening a book on it, if they hit you over the head with it. There is a wealth of material on this. Rich. Beyond me.[8]

What would happen that would facilitate Pan-Africanism in the Caribbean islands is that there emerged in the Caribbean islands a free man. This was because the British brought technicians boatwrights, blacksmiths, wheelwrights, people to repair the sugar mills who were low-bred, scurvy. Whites who had no social states in England. Now they are on an island with all these lush and plush black women and a shortage of white people. They had status that they never had before. They drank better liquor than they ever had before. They lived in better houses than they ever had before. They had servants which they never had before. However, instead of fixing sugar mills and being blacksmiths, they said yes to all temptations, and some of them died of just sheer exhaustion. If any man is fool enough to think that he can satisfy every available women, you should put him in an insane asylum right away and tell him he might have better luck drinking all the water in the sea.[9]

That's how some of these Whites died out. The significant thing is that Blacks learned their craft as their helpers, took over their jobs, and became the masters of the sugar mills, the boat menders, and created a separate technical class in the Caribbean. They had now enough voice and importance to demand better treatment as slaves and later on almost freedom to the last man.

This Caribbean freeman, a thinking class, began to contact free Africans in New England. These Africans in New England had become free approximately for some of the same reasons. In New England the weather was so bad, there was no point in keeping a slave all the year round when you could only use him six months. You had the industrial slave, carpenters, plasterers, housebuilders. You could rent him for four dollars a day, and sometimes you gave him one dollar. He could work on Saturday and Sunday, and that money all went to him. Since there were no great demands on him for farm work, he could work his way out of slavery. Which they often did. A lot of the escaped slaves also came to the North.

We developed a class of freemen in the United States who made contact with the freemen in the Caribbean islands. As two people, we weren't as stupid as we are today always telling about how different we were and how many servants we had we worked together. The Caribbeans didn't call themselves Caribbeans, and we didn't call ourselves Americans. We all knew one thing that you have forgotten. That all of us left African on the same slave ships. The slave ships stopped at some islands and left some captives in the Caribbean. Then they came to America and dropped us off. All of us took names based on where the slave ships put us down. Slave ships didn't bring any Trinidadians, any Barbadians, any Jamaicans, any high-yellows or low-yellows, no Deltas, and no AKA's. We weren't into that nonsense at that time, and so, because we came together as a sane people, we were on missions together.

The Colonization Movement during the first half of the nineteenth century with the establishment of Liberia—with missionary societies going to different parts of Africa, especially Sierra Leone and Liberia—was an equal enterprise for Caribbean people and Black Americans working side by side and hand in hand. Nobody's calling any names. Nobody's playing any damn fool.

Under this condition, all Pan-Africans. Prince Hall from Barbados came and established the Black Masons. He didn't go around shouting, "Look you people have been here. I had to come all the way and establish your Black Masons. You Black Americans have been sitting on your behind waiting for me." No nonsense like that. No nonsense that some Garveyists have today. It is said, "Garvey came to Black America and found the Black Americans with a wishbone and gave him a backbone." That's a damn lie.

We had fought and built more independent institutions than any African people ever built outside of Africa before Garvey got here and before the Caribbean migration started. This just happens to be a matter of truth. We had to do ti. We couldn't get any other people. If we were going to have any institutions, we were going to build them ourselves. We did it out of circumstances.

Let's go back to the first half of the nineteenth century. I'm saying that this was Pan-Africanism, and the whole of the nineteenth century was world Pan-Africanism. The African colonial revolts were Pan-Africanism. The continuation of the fight in the Caribbean was a form of Pan-Africanism. The massive slave revolts in the first half were a form of Pan-Africanism. Each one of us, trying to get back what slavery and colonialism had taken away. Later on, Richard Allen and James Varick got tired of going into Jim Crow churches and established churches that were ours alone. What did they call them? The African Methodist Episcopal Church and the African Methodist Episcopal Zion Church. If they were afraid of Africa, why did they call it an African name? If the great Barbadian prince Hall was afraid of Africa, when he founded the Black Masons why didn't he call it the Black Masons? He called it the African Lodge.

Our first comedians called themselves the African rascals or the Ethiopian clowns. My definition is that any attempt to regain what has been lost, taken away, or misinterpreted is a form of Pan-Africanism. In the midst of all of this in the second half of the nineteenth century when we had pseudo-democracy for a little while, before it was betrayed, we developed maybe the most independent of our many independent religious institutions, the Baptist Church.

The Baptist Church is the most African of all of the

churches that we have developed. Now, I didn't say they were sanitarily pure. I grew up a Baptist. I taught Sunday school. I think sometimes, in my anger, the Baptist Church is the loudest, the wrongest, and the most corrupt of them all. Still, I think it's the most African in its manifestation. Not because of the corruption. But because there are so many things African still being practiced in that church. Some things are practiced wrongly. Some things are being practiced opportunistically. When I saw may stepmother being buried in that church where she grew up, and I knew that she was one of the most evil women to ever walk the earth. And we said, "She will never die." One day the Devil and God are going to let her evil away. There was a whole community that she had slandered, singing her praises; people whose reputations she had destroyed, praising her name. Now that she is dead, all is forgiven. That's a beautiful cultural trait. I'm afraid I'm not quite big enough to forgive. Well, anyway, it's a beautiful thing. The point is that having attended funerals, wakes, and weddings in Africa, I know that behavior is pure African.

At the end of the nineteenth century, we had been fighting all over the world, one way or another. The colonial wars had been fought all over Africa—the Zulu wars, the Ashanti wars in Ghana, the wars led by Muslims, the Mahdi wars in the Sudan, wars led by Moslem rebels from the territory. You do not understand that all over the world we had already established a fighting revolutionary heritage before we entered the twenty-first century. You let a bunch of nobodies come and try to teach us revolution when we've had so much revolution we could can it, put it on the shelf, and sell it.

In Brazil, African revolutionists had brought two nations into being: Palmares and Bahia. Many of the Africans coming into Brazil by-passed the auction block, knocked over the auctioneer, went to the forest, and absolutely never were slaves. The country is so big, and the forest is so deep you could never find them. And some of them; are still there. Go up the river in Guyana and you will find some Africans who are still there practicing Africans customs and speaking an African language. They tell their children never be bothered with gold because gold makes White men crazy. It might make you crazy.

At the end of this nineteenth century with the American fight, Booker T. Washington made his Cotton States Exposition Speech (Atlanta, 1895). Du Bois began his ascent. The fight for a constitution in the Caribbean islands. The fight to regain the land in Africa. We had been fighting allover the world, even in the Pacific. On one island, Tasmania, the British had destroyed every man, woman, and child. At the end of this century, a Trinidadian lawyer looking at all of this struggle decieded to put a name on this struggle. This was not the beginning of it, but the intellectual beginning of it. In an informal sense, it had been going on for three hundred years.[10]

In my opinion, Pan-Africanism began when an unknown African, being pushed toward a slave ship, picked up a handful of dirt and put it in his mouth. Then he looked back as his beloved land was disappearing behind him. I say that was the first Pan-Africanist. He was longing for the land and the freedom that was being taken away. Near the end of the century, H. Sylvester Williams put a name to it and called conference in London (1900). Du Bois attended the conference. Many of the Africans who just happened to be in London attended the conference. They had no money to sent for anybody from anyplace. If Africans got there, they just happened to be there. But they got the conference underway.

They didn't ask for African independence. They asked for an improvement in African education so that Africans could be eventually in a position to rule themselves. A modest demand. I don't see why that should have frightened anybody. After the conference, H. Sylvester, involved in the whole constitutional right in the Caribbean, no longer had the energy or the time.

Look at what happened then that probably can't happen now because of the stupid argument between us.

H. Sylvester Williams literally turned to Du Bois and said, "The ball's in your court." Du Bois would handle the Pan-African concept until we got to the fifth conference. He would go and have the first large conference in Paris (1919). He would go to a Senegalese, Blaise Diagne, then France's minister of colonies. I don't mean assistant minister of Colonies. I mean minister of colonies. Blaise had delivered 500,000 troops to the French during World War I. The Senegalese turned those Germans back. The Germans had said that this African was the greatest hand-to-hand combat fighter the world had ever known. They said you see a Senegalese coming, try to kill him before he gets to you because if he gets his hands on you, it'll be too late to say your prayers. They literally helped to build the French empire.

So when Blaise Diagne goes to Georges Clemenceau, the Prime Minister of France, and asks for permission to hold that conference for Du Bois, Clemenceau is not in a position to say no. Not to this powerful blackman. he said, "Go ahead and hold your conference." However, there was not too much publicity about it. The conference was held. Subcommittees of the conference were held in Belguim. A great radical journalist decided the conference was not the important action going. William Monroe Trotter came to Paris, argued with Du Bois and said, "The action is not here. The action is at Versailes." Trotter went to Versailles and burst into a meeting.[11]

There were the heads of the world, the winners and losers of the war. They were sitting at Versailles trying to make a treaty for the White world when this little Black man from Boston burst into that conference and pointed his fingers at his President Woodrow Wilson and said, "Don't betray us again. You're going to have a second world war if you betray us again."

Wilson ordered that he be instantaneously thrown out.

Clemenceau reminded President Wilson, "I'm the host and I want to hear what the chap has to say." He stood there, lectured for one hour and ten minutes. I'm sorry they didn't have tape recorders in those days. William Monroe Trotter had more nerve than sense. He came from the aristocratic class, too. One of people of the "light brigade." He could have walked out of the Black race at any time. He was light enough to pass the "taxi-cab test." He could get a cab downtown late at night, and yet he chose to fight. After they threw him out and he realized he didn't have enough money to get back to America, he hired himself on a tramp steamer washing dished all the way back. When they discovered who he was, they took down the clean dishes and made him wash them. The book about Trotter is not so well written, but the incident is in the book.

DuBois would find other conferences and we would continue through World War I and World War II. At the end of World War II, Caribbeans, Africans, and Black Americans came together. From Africa came Peter Abrahams; Garvey's first wife, Amy Ashwood; Nnamdi Azikiwe from Nigeria; Johnstone Kenyatta, who would later be known as Jomo Kenyatta; W.E.B. Du Bois; a young African student once known as Francis N. Nkrumah, now Kwame Nkrumah; one of the conveners—George Padmore, the brains behind the whole thing—would later write its official history. This conference laid the basis for the African Independence Explosion that would take place in 1957 with the independence of Ghana.

What I'm trying to say in closing is that Pan-Africanism has always been a part of our lives and we have moved away from our salvation to the extent that we have forgotten Pan-Africanism. Integration has been a disaster because integration wasn't our greatest need. Justice was our greatest need. Once you get justice, who you integrate with socially is a personal matter which has nothing to do with law. Where you send your child to school depends on the needs of your child and your interpretation of those needs.

Wherever the school is, you'll find a way to get the child there and in that case no one should have the right to keep him/her from there. The schools in your own community should be well kept, and if there's a school outside of the community teaching something they need for their survival, no one should be able to keep them from it. You should continue to build the schools in your own community concurrent with the demands of the right to go to other schools if there is something there your child needs. We have misinterpreted this.

Now, as we face the twenty-first century, we have to understand. We have to make certain radical changes in our lives and our attitudes. We must stop being consumers of everything. All production does not require high tech. A first year chemistry student with a 'B' average can make good toothpaste, so why are you letting *Colgate* do for you what a dummy can do? You don't even have to be brilliant. I can make soap and I'm about as untechnical as a person can be.

We have to start taking care of these basic things. We've got young men involved in a stupid war that no one can win, solely because we did not make a place for them in our own community. Had we had factories in our community, just small factories manufacturing T-shirts, shoes, shoelaces, eyeglasses, some of them would have been managing these plants. Then they would go home to everloving young ladies. Some of them would be good husbands in our neighborhoods, bringing families together, taking little children to the park and boasting about it.

Men like to look at the reflection of themselves in a child. "That's my daughter. That's my boy." They like that. You don't know how many men who desert children really love them. Not being able to do their best infringes upon their manhood to the point where they take flight.

We have to build from within. We have to reach out to

Africa and Africa has to reach out to us. The silly reason between Caribbean people and Black Americans has to come to an end. The poor attitudes of some Africans toward both of us must come to an end. We are a billion people on the face of this earth and maybe all we need, first and foremost, is each other. We pose no threat to the world. Coming to power, we have no plans to bomb other people's cities. We have no plans to build a Black branch of the Ku Klux Klan. We will not use our energy in such a stupid way.

Once we come to our own realization of our own responsibility and regain the concept and the idea of nation, the concept of entrepreneurship is going to go with it. Then we will listen to Booker T. Washington and take from him what we need and the things we do not need, we'll just leave along. We will take from W.E.B. Du Bois the political lessons that we need. We will take from Marcus the lessons in the African connection that we need. We don't have go be Muslim to take form Elijah Muhammad and Malcolm X the lessons about the first nation away from home that we need. We don't have to believe in non-violence to recognize that Martin Luther King, Jr. was, among other things, one of the great theologians of the twentieth century. We can take spiritual lessons from him and reject non-violence. He can still be of value to us.

The answer for our salvation is within ourselves. Europe has no answer for us. For the European all of the things he has announced to the world have failed for him. And you are sad indeed to think it will succeed for you. Socialism has failed for him because he never really tried it. Christianity has failed for him because he never really believed in it. Capitalism has failed for him because he overplayed it and never really had any humanity in relationship to it. You can do better than this, but whatsoever you choose as a way of life, you have to re-write, remold it, reshape it to suit your case.

You cannot adopt any ideology that says, "Religion is the

opiate of the people." Mankind has not grown to the point where he can do without some kind of spirituality. Personally, I don't think religions as such are a necessity. But I think and know spirituality is essential to existence on the face of the earth. It is spirituality that makes man higher than the dog. Once we look at ourselves this way, once we begin to practice the essential selfishness of survival, once we find our number one ally by finding a mirror. Look into that mirror and see what's staring back at you. Say to that ally, "You and I will change the whole world. You and I will make a difference. You and I will walk this earth respecting the manhood and the womanhood of everything under God's creation and demand the same thing for ourselves." That's tomorrow's work. When you are serious about tomorrow's work, you always start it today.

Chapter Five

The Historical Basis of Africancentricity
April 3, 1992

I will go immediately to the point. I will let you know exactly who I do not have a fight with. I do not have a fight with Molefi Asante. I have a fight with his generation. His generation has failed to see the latitude and the longitude of the subject that was already old when Professor Asante's parents were born. His generation had made a cult around something that is an intellectual exercise that is supposed to be continuously investigated. The jury is always out on intellectual subjects because the investigation is always ongoing.[1]

I have an argument with the word "Afrocentricity" because it is a compromise with the word Africa. There is no "fro" in Africa. You have no problem saying Italian American or German American. Now, if you don't like any hyphenated American, just say African.

What we're talking about is either Africancentricity or it is nothing. What we are talking about is what I have been referring to as African consciousness all along. I have no argument with the books of Molefi Asante. He has given us a good analysis of what he calls Afrocentricity. He has done the spade work so that a different kind of scholar will come later and take it a step further. That is the role of scholarship to take scholarship one step further from where the scholar has found it. I'm going to

---

tell you an old story. Then I'm going to get to work.

Years ago I was changing planes in Denver and I saw a former student across the way approaching me. I could tell by the fabric that he didn't buy his suit in any bargain basement. He was in the anti-poverty program. But he was not from a poverty-ridden family. He just hung out with the anti-poverty kids and he had sat on the front seat in class.

I couldn't tell whether he was smiling or smirking. In school I had told the story of Imhotep and Africa's contribution to medicine and all of Africa's other contribution. I told him about the myth of Arab Science. What we call Arab Science is really Egyptian Science which has been stolen and re-written by the Arabs. You can tell right now that I have an anti-Arab prejudice. I just don't like them.

I asked him, "What are you doing here in Denver?" He said, "I live here. I went to medical school here. I'm a physician here." "When I was in medical school," he said, "I would tell my colleagues all these medical stories you told me about Imhotep, his multi-genius, and I would tell them as though it was my story. I didn't even give you any credit. I'm sorry about that." I told him, "You could have stolen from a second-rater. If you're going to steal, steal from the best." I asked him what he was doing there. He said, "I am a Professor of Abdominal Medicine, University of Denver. I also hold the same position at Denver General Hospital." Then I had to run for my plane and he had to run for his car.

My point is that when you impact on a life this is what the teacher is supposed to do, but the teacher doesn't know what the hell he/she is doing the teacher plays God without a halo and without a Bible. When you throw out a theory, you never know where it's going to go. We have to be careful with what we do and what we say. We have responsibility.

My argument is about latitude and longitude. We haven't kicked what we call "Afrocentricity" back far enough. We haven't dealt with its historical roots. Its historical roots are as long as the disturbance of African people by foreigners and the pulling of them out of their land. When I look at "Afrocentricity" I'm not arguing against Molefi Asante. I'm looking at it through my experience. After all, I'm a product of the Harlem History Club of the 1930's. Arthur Schomburg taught me the interrelationship of African history to world history. Willis N. Huggins taught me the political meaning of history. William Leo Hansberry, in his lectures when he came over from Howard, taught me the philosophical meaning of history.[2]

I came to New York at a time when a great cadre of Caribbean activists who wouldn't be heard in the Caribbean world of their day or this day because the Caribbeans don't hear intellects at home. The intellects have to go away from home to be heard. They are tigers abroad and meek Moses at home. When I came to New York, Raphael Powell had already written his book *Human Side of a People and their Right Name*. This is Africancentricity. He disputed whether people had a right to slap the word "Negro" on a people who never heard of the word and didn't choose the word for themselves. This is Africancentricity.[3]

The Harlem Renaissance, at its best, was a form of Africancentricity. Look at Arthur Schomburg's work, "The Negro Digs Up His Past." Look at some of the best work, even the folklore of Zora Neale Hurston. The folklore tells us something about Africancentricity. It's our way of looking at things different from other people. It is our point of view, our window on the world, our vantage point based on our view from that window.[4]

This is just a little bit of Zora Neale who I knew. She was as crazy as a loon. I loved her just the same. There was a man who died in the Johnstown Flood in Pennsylvania. So he got to heaven. He was telling his story and all the angels were listening. There was an old man pooh-poohing everything. When it was all over, the man asked, "Who is this old man? I'm telling my story about the great flood in Johnstown, and he doesn't seem to believe anything?" Somebody said, "Now that's Brother Noah. He can really tell you about a flood." That's Africancentricity folklore. Don't think about Africancentricity as something narrow, it is our way of looking at things, feeling about things.

It even used to be our way of courtship. We have lost everything imitating people who don't know where they are going. There used to be a time when a man would come into the house and he had to have a "story" ready. Even if she was amenable, you had to have a "story" because she would ask you, "What's your story?" You'd better have a story ready. So you had one ready. Even if it was a lie. You told her something. You don't just say, "Come here gal." Even in courtship we developed a technique of verbal approaches which were a form of Africancentricity in approach.[5]

Even the father the first visit he looks you over slightly and the second visit he looks you over again. However, on the third visit she's a little late and you're sitting in the living room with the father. The father talks about a whole lot of things and then he finally comes to the point. "Son, what's your intentions toward my daughter? Can you support her? What kind of job have you got?" That's Africancentricity in the protection of his daughter.[6]

You think Africancentricity is a narrow thing. It is as broad as our view of the world. Let's look at its origins and its roots. By my interpretation, the first inkling of Africancentricity is when Africans being forced on a boat, became conscious of the loss of their homeland. In essence, Africancentricity was any effort on the part of a person of African descent attempting to reclaim what slavery and colonialism took away.

We're talking about a five-hundred-year struggle to get back what slavery and colonialism took away. We're talking about men who made a decision on the boat that they'd rather jump over and feed the sharks rather than go into slavery.

We're talking about the terrible revolutionary struggle on the plantations in the Caribbean Islands. Many times on those plantations the African craftsman made a cutlass and then made a stabbing weapon on the side and slipped it to the slaves in the field to start the revolution. That, too, is Africancentricity.[7]

We're also talking about the Haitian Revolution when Boukman called for a Black heaven. He said if he met his white slavemaster at the Pearly Gates, that he would slay him right in front of the angel Gabriel. Also, we're talking about Mackandal, the other priest who came before Boukman.[8]

What angers me about the whole approach to Africancentricity is the fact that it is so narrow. It is part of our totality as a people. It is part of our style as a people. It began to develop in this African Holocaust and it hasn't ended. It has continued in its progression.

Early in the nineteenth century that progression came to a crescendo. In the Caribbean Islands slave revolts had reached their peak. In Brazil and the rest of South America, it had reached its peak. In the New England states of the United States, slavery was not functioning profitably because the weather was too cold. There was no point in keeping the slave all the year round. You could only work him six months. So the industrial slave developed. This industrial slave learned to read. He was a plasterer. He was a plumber. He learned faster than many of those dumb Whites coming from Europe, got better jobs, and sometimes got better treatment. Africans began to read, write, and publish newspapers. Frederick Douglass would come into that kind of atmosphere which was created before Douglass came into existence.

Frederick Douglass was only marginally an Africancentrist. The men around him were Africancentrists. Douglass wasn't conservative in the slightest. He was as pure a radical as you could find. He thought that the center of the fight against slavery and oppression was right here in the U.S.A. He felt that we had worked and slaved here and therefore let us resolve this here. That Africa would be given consideration after that solution.

He was neither right nor wrong. This was a point of view that Douglass projected. The men around him did not fight him over that point of view. This was because we had produced in the nineteenth century men and women who could differ with you. It's almost like pacing you in a race. They run beside you in order to encourage you to run even faster. But they weren't trying to knock you out of the race, knowing that you were the better racer. They were there to make you continue to be a better racer.[9]

Now people get in to destroy you because we have a different kind of mentality. That first half of the nineteenth century in the United States was the birth of literary Africancentricity. There were the newspapers. Martin R. Delany, David Walker, and three massive slave revolts. At the same time a literature of the possibility of a state was developing in the Caribbean Islands. Plus a minor and a major literature later on.[10]

A literature was developing in Africa. But into Africa during the same period would go Edward Wilmot Blyden, a young man from the Virgin Islands who would become the finest African mind of the nineteenth century. His inaugural address at Liberia College (1881) is the purest form of intellectual Africancentricity. His address on liberal education for Blacks was not only ahead of his time, it's ahead of this time.

> . . . we shall be obliged to work for sometime to come, not only without popular sympathy which we think our due, but with utterly inadequate resources.
> . . . Too many times we fancy that we must feed grist into other people's mills. We strive to be those things most unlike ourselves. In feeding the grist to other people's mills, of course, nothing comes out except what has been put in. That then is our great sorrow.[11]

Henry Highland Garnet would go to Jamaica to rest up from the wars in the United States because the activists of Jamaica had enough freedom to invite him. When he discovered that the condition in the United States had not changed, he thanked the Jamaican hosts and said, in effect, "I'm returning to the United States. Not to ask for justice because I do not expect it. Not to ask for integration because I do not want it. I'm returning to the United States to devote the rest of my life in the effort to tear that republic down."

Black men don't speak that way anymore. Black men don't have that kind of outrage anymore. We better look at this nineteenth century Black man all over the world. Let's take a holistic view of him. We'd better warm our hands at his fire before we go into the twenty-first century. He has some courage we have not regained or looked into.

When we came to the middle of the nineteenth century here, there was the debate over slavery. In the Caribbean Islands there was the debate over Constitution and in Africa there were the debates over the colonial forms. These were all forms of Africancentricity. I consider Africancentricity: any sincere effort on the part of African people (literally or militarily) to regain what slavery and colonialism took away and to restore the nation as you originally conceived it to be.

We are talking about something that is very broad. It's broader than its creditor. We must take Molefi Asante's baby, change its diaper, change its diet, and teach it to grow up. Molefi may not know it, but the child will become a man or a woman, and the child will open the door for the freedom still to come and "for the beautiful ones not yet born."

We have looked too narrowly on the things that have influenced our lives. We don't have to leave the church to be revolutionary because the church was revolutionary. Some people toned it down. We don't even have to stop being

Moslem. We can turn that into a revolutionary event as opposed to an Arab-loving slave cult. We have to study it first.

I've yet to meet a Black Islamic scholar. Not one. I've met scholars who are scholars of their religion. If you understand the religion, you would understand that, too, has Africancentricity. The Black side was Africancentricity.

Study the life of Mohammed Ahmed of the Sudan. Study the life of Ben Abdullah Hassan, called the "Mad Mullah" of Somalia, who drove out the British. Study the life of these African rebels. You want to be Africancentrists? Study the life of the greatest scholar to come out of Islam, Ahmed Baba. He was the author of forty-seven books, each on a separate subject. He told his students, "Believe in God and Science." When they exiled him to Morocco, he wrote two books in Morocco, in which he tried to explain his country to those dumb North African Arabs. I'm saying that before this man was Moslem, he was Africancentric. His religion did not rule out his nationalistic commitment to his people. If I dealt with Africancentricity in the latter part of the twentieth century, I would speak indefinitely. However, I'm not going to do that, because I'm going to stop in a little while.[12]

Malcolm X was as much an Africancentrist as anybody could be. If you listen to King properly, so was he. You're always starting fights where there are no fights. To have a system, call it Afrocentricity, and not put W.E.B. Du Bois at the center of it in the twentieth century is not to have it at all.

Now, Du Bois was hard to take. I had three encounters with Du Bois. He didn't believe that anybody who did not finish a whole lot of college had anything worth listening to. When I sat with him and discussed Kant, great men of letters in history, and the philosophy of the categorical imperative, all the philosophical ways of life of the world of Africa and Asia and difference religions of the world, he said, "Son, are you sure you didn't finish Morehouse?" I just had to finish something. I said, "Dr. Du Bois,

I didn't finish the seventh grade." I finished the first part of the seventh grade. I can't remember all the different honorary degrees I've got. I've got two more coming up in the next month or so. I've got more books than are in most libraries and I understand most of them.

I'm saying that as we came into the twentieth century, Du Bois had behind him the first Africancentric approach to slavery, *The Suppression of the African Slave Trade in the United States.* As we moved into the twentieth century, the first Africancentric approach to urban sociology, *The Philadelphia Negro, The Souls of Black Folk,* and *The Gift of Black Folk* were already behind him. His little book, *The Negro,* was the first overall survey of Africans in world history. He never brought to his books on history the technique that he brought to his absolute greatest Africancentric book, from the point of view of technique of writing and research, *Black Reconstruction.* Professor Asante should never have used "fro" in the first place. Because there is no "fro" in Africa. Who called it a Black Studies program in the first place? Maybe the word Africa should have been used from the beginning.[13]

Forget that. We look at everybody's history. Where were we? The same as my own searching as a child. Looking in the Bible and seeing all those white faces, all those angels. Not a single little black or brown angel. They would tell God is love. God is merciful. God is a respecter of kith and kin. You mean He didn't let one little Brown or Black angel sneak into heaven and he tells me He's love? I ain't going to buy that.

All I'm trying to say, in these not too organized few words, is that Africancentricity needs to be looked at historically and broadside. We need to look at some of our neglected writers. We need to look at John Blassingame's *The Slave Community* and Sterling Stuckey's *Slave Culture.* Africancentricity has been a lot of things. We need to look at literary Africancentricity. We need to look at Margaret Walker's *Jubilee.* Don't neglect James

Baldwin's *Go Tell It On The Mountain*. This is religious Africancentricity.[14]

Don't just look in little small corners. Africancentricity is as big as we are. It is part of the sum, the substance, and the stimulation that will shock us out of our lethargy and make us see the people we have been and create the people we still can be. It will transfer to our children the will to make the whole new human society.

That is the mission and that is the legacy we leave. Not only for our children. We leave it for all children.

Chapter Six

Education for a New Reality in the African World

National Alliance of Black Educators
New York, NY
November 19, 1985

On occasions like this when I'm trying to decide whether I'm listening to an introduction or an obituary, I know it's a long way from that farmer's field in Union Springs, Alabama. I measure the years and go immediately to the subject.

My subject, "Education for a New Reality in the African World," was not easily chosen. I have spoken on this subject or some aspect of it many times over the years. I have exhausted my arguments in favor of the subject without losing my passion for the subject. Certain local events, certain recent events in the world have renewed my anger over the subject. We still do not understand the importance of education because education is power.

When education is properly done, education opens the door for power. One of the things that we fail to understand is that our oppressor cannot afford to educate us. We live in a society where, if we are properly educated, we will not ask for power. We will take power. We have to locate African people on the map of human geography. We will have to stop answering by names that our mothers and fathers did not give us. We will have to stop answering to names of which we are not.[1]

There is a real crisis facing Black educators. This crisis began a long time ago with things we did not understand. I think, in reading about a scene of an African being forced on a slave ship, and he reached back and puts a handful of African dirt in his mouth, I think he understood more about education, more than most of us understand. He understood the basis of a nation: land. Until we understand the land basis of education and the nation basis of education, we will miss the point. Now where we have to go looking at education is to what extent our approach to education went wrong and to when we stopped being innovators and became imitators. That basically is what this speech is all about.[2]

In the nineteenth century we began to be "those things most unlike ourselves." When we had the golden opportunity to set a new tone in education, we tried to be like our oppressor instead of setting a new basis for education. In fact, true education has one purpose, one purpose alone, that is to train the student to be a handler of power. If nothing more than handling the power over him and herself. Everything else is a waste of time.[3]

Power consists of control and understanding the elements of control. We have to look back at how we came under control and how during the fifteenth and sixteenth centuries Europe locked us into what Professor Ivan Van Sertima calls the "five-hundred-year room." Into this five-hundred-year room of history the European not only colonized the world, they colonized information about the world. Understand also the Europeans had to come out of a seven-hundred-year room.

After the decline of Rome, for seven hundred years Europe was penned into Europe and had to fight a war against the so-called infidel Arabs. The fear of the "infidel" Arabs and Islam barred Europe from the Mediterranean. Europe, feeding on itself (a poor diet, indeed) went into the Middle Ages, and Europe had to restore its confidence. Europe restored its confidence and rebuilt its fortunes at the expense of African and Asian people. You have to understand how Europe came out of its misery at our expense, built the so-called New World, and rebuilt its economy by placing us into that five-hundred-year-room.

The basis of education for a new reality is to pull us out of this five-hundred-year-room. We have to understand what went wrong with our education and to understand the nineteenth century in the African world. The nineteenth century in the African world may have been the greatest century in the whole of the African world outside of Africa. This might be the century that we have to go back to and understand in order to survive in the twentieth and twenty-first centuries. We produced the finest minds that we have produced since the decline of Egypt and Nile Valley Civilization in the nineteenth century.[4]

We produced the rebels, the mentality, the realists in that nineteenth century. This is the century of Frederick Douglass and Martin Delany. This is the century of the great ministers who tower over Martin Luther King, Jr. and were more realistic than a Martin Luther King, Jr. Taking nothing from King, this is the century of Henry Highland Garnet whose motto was "Resistance, Resistance, Resistance." This is the century of a search for Africa again. This is the century of the great black women, Sojourner Truth and Harriet Tubman. We have forgotten that century. We will not orient ourselves in the twentieth century until we go back to that century. And I'm just taking about the United States. Now let's go back to the Caribbean Islands.[5]

When we look at the Caribbean Islands, there is a century of physical resistance. Let us go back to South America, especially Brazil, where Blacks brought into being two Black nations. This is where Blacks arriving from Africa by-passed the auction block, went into the hinterlands and formed African nations. Palmares lasted for 110 years. Bahai lasted almost as long. Where dimensions of African cultural continuity produced the most successful slave revolts in the history of the world, mostly in Jamaica. When we look at Jamaica and Haiti, you will wonder why, if Jamaica fought longer and harder, why is it that Haiti brought off an independent state and Jamaica did not?

Haiti fought over a shorter period with a greater degree of consistency. And when Haiti hit the French at a strategic time when Napolean was so involved with other European campaigns, they could bring it off successfully. When the Jamaicans were fighting, too much time lapsed between their revolutions and the British could destabilize them. Jamaicans had to remount each revolution from scratch. The time-lapse did not give them the facility to bring forth a nation. While the total of the Haitian revolutions (there were more than one) happened over a twenty-year period.[6]

Let us examine the nineteenth century over and over again, all over the world, especially the Caribbean Islands. When you look at the Caribbean Islands today, you can look at the leadership in the Caribbean Islands and write every single one of them off as lost. They're all copouts to American colonialism or English colonialism. But don't write the people off. Remember, those specks of dust in the Caribbean once challenged Europe and changed the geography of this hemisphere. Because of the challenge of the Caribbean Islands—Toussaint L' Ouverture, Jean-Jacques Dessalines, and Christophe Napolean had to sell the Lousiana Territory. These Caribbean revolutions brought into being the stimulation for the massive slave revolts in the United States.

I don't know of one successful curriculum in a single Black Studies program in this country that realistically teaches courses on resistance in the Caribbean islands and the African world in the nineteenth century. I mounted one, but all of my courses are oversubscribed. And only the least number of students could understand what I was trying to get at.

Let's turn to this nineteenth century and let's talk about this Caribbean mind and its contribution to the stimulation of Black social forms in the nineteenth century. Also, we need to understand the Caribbean mind never functioned well at home. Once the Caribbean mind functioned well at home, it is driven away from home. Most of these minds left home and the best of these minds came to the United States. It started with Prince Hall. Robert Campbell would come here. He would travel with Martin Delany to Africa and write *A Search for a Place*. John B. Russwurm would edit *Freedom's Journal*. Peter Ogden was one of the founders of the Odd Fellows. Prince Hall would found the Masons. Why didn't these minds function at home? They didn't function at home then. They can't function at home now. You can trace it two hundred years through Garvey and those who went home and were killed, including Walter Rodney.[7]

The greatest and clearest of these minds of the nineteenth century was Edward Wilmot Blyden. What he said about education in his famous inaugural address at Liberia College in 1881 said more about education over one hundred years ago than we are saying right now. He said:

> We will have to work for many years to come. Not only without the popular support that we must have, but with inadequate resources.
> ... We strive to be those things most unlike ourselves. No matter what talent we have, we feed grist into other people's mills ... and, of course, nothing comes out except what has been put in. And that then is our great sorrow.[8]

That was in 1881, over one hundred years ago. It was not only ahead of that time, it's ahead of this time. We're still doing it. He was one of the finest voices of the nineteenth century.

Now, let's look at Africa in the nineteenth century and the massive anti-colonial revolts. This is the century when the African world faced reality as it has never faced reality before. In the first half of that century, Africans began a physical revolt. The Zulu Wars in Southern Africa had already started. The Ashanti Wars in Ghana had already started. The Islamic Wars in the Sudan had already started. The Maji Maji Wars in Tanganyika and neighboring territories, the Riff Wars in North Africa had already started. And the wars in Nigeria led by Ousmane Dan Fodio had already started.[9]

The physical confrontation diminished as the slave trade turned into colonialism (another from of slavery) and the Africans also noticed the missionary effort was also a form of slavery. The Europeans began to take away the African energies and began to destroy the African images of God.

One of the ways of enslaving you, after they remove one set of chains and put the chains on the mind, is to not only change your religion, but also to make you abandon your religion, make you change your dress and to laugh at your gods. Once you change to their gods, their dress, their tastes, their music, their food, they don't need any prison walls after that. They've got prison walls more binding, because the prison wall is inside of your mind.[10]

Once we face the reality of the imprisonment of the African mind in the nineteenth century, we will face up to what was happening to that mind. We will look at the Black convention movement, look at the debates between Blacks and Blacks and look at the Blacks going to Liberia to "Christianize" their "heathen" brothers. Read Alexander Crummell's work. Alexander Crummell was a great Black missionary. But Alexander Crummell was a missionary with the mentality of a white missionary. He was going to spread Christianity in a continent where every element that went originally into the making of Christianity, Islam and

Judaism began. All of it started in Africa, one way or the other.[11]

In my research, I read a dissertation on this, written by an African at Syracuse University. He was thrown out of Syracuse University, of course, in 1933. His dissertation dealt with the fact why African religions never became world religions. He said no pew, no collection plate, no temples, no missionaries. Everything is free. How can such a religion become a world religion? Nobody is exploiting anybody. Priests are free. The community pay the priests so they don't have to pass the hat. The community brings the priest his food, makes his clothes. All of the elements that you call Christianity came out of Africa. All of the symbols came out of Africa. He pointed out that when the Jews came into Africa, they had no clear religion, law, or language and when they left and took their exodus they had all three. So you knew he was going to get thrown out.

During the second half of the nineteenth century in the Caribbean Island, the revolts were taking off, except the Haitian. The missionary-educated African activists were taking over. The bulk of rebels were coming to the fore. In this country new institutions were coming into being: land grant colleges, new approaches to education . . . some of them imaginative. At the end of the nineteenth century we saw the emergence of Booker T. Washington. Here we need to tarry because here is where we might have gone wrong.[12]

Booker T. Washington's speech (Atlanta Cotton Exposition, held in Atlanta, 1895) was misunderstood then and it is misunderstood now. It was a speech of strategy. All strategy does not work all the time. It was one of the most unique con games ever played. He spoke to the white South, the black South, the North and he got what he wanted and what he needed. He maneuvered to appeal to all sides. No one really noticed. There was a reporter from Boston who noticed that some of the Blacks who came down from the balcony were crying and some of them waved their hands to where Booker T. Washington was standing. They shook their heads and said, "Oh, no, Booker, no, Booker." Some of them began their retreat out of the South. They began the migration because they couldn't believe some of the things that he had said. Yet, he had set a pace. He had taken Blacks out of the nineteenth and into the twentieth century.[3]

We didn't quite understand what he had done. The South misinterpreted the speech. They thought that this meant that he endorsed segregation. In the five-year span from 1895 to 1900, a rash of Jim Crow laws came into being. That wasn't his intent or what he meant. Now the debate between W.E.B. Du Bois and Booker T. Washington started and we started choosing sides. We started choosing sides and we haven't straightened it out yet. We assumed that we had to choose sides between political/liberal education and agrarian/industrial education: either Du Bois was right or Booker T. Washington was right. Both of them were right.[4]

Both of them looked at the world based on how they were reared. Du Bois was raised in New England, a partial aristocrat. You could be aristocrat in New England and not have any money. Washington was a farm boy from slave parents and he didn't know his father. Therefore, he looked at the world that way. Both men were practical based on each one's vantage point in looking at the world. We needed what both men offered. We needed it at that time and we need it now.

Booker T. Washington's program would have eventually led us to Du Bois' program and Du Bois' program would have eventually led us to a consideration of Washington's program. We did not have to reject either one of them. At the time when Whites weren't paying much attention to our education, we could have innovated to the point of creating an education system that would have moved ahead of American education. However, instead of leading we began to follow, and today we are following a people who don't know where they are going.

We have not considered that.

The education for White people in this country is basically bad and even worse for us because it is not an education for our reality. If we followed Booker T. Washington's education, there wouldn't be a boarded-up house in any black community in this country. There would be Black plumbers, Black carpenter, Blacks who owned brickyards, and Black technicians who would fix the house long before it reaches the point of even being boarded-up.

Had we followed W.E.B. Du Bois' program, there would be no inept Black politicians because we would have learned how to make our politicians account to us, or else remove them. So we could have had a wedding between what Booker T. Washington was saying and what Du Bois was saying. They were saying that Washington was a traditionalist and Du Bois was a modernist. But there was no conflict between one and the other.

Early in this century, the Caribbean mind began to produce the concept called Pan-Africanism. The Caribbean mind has a way of producing seeds that do not grow in the soil of the Caribbean. These seed grew in the soil of the U.S. This was a new international education that few of us understood the full dimension of: the idea of bringing the totality of the African world together as one people looking at the total peopleness of African people. When Sylvester Williams called his first Pan-African Conference together in London in 1900, he had tried a Pan-African league in Trinidad. It had failed in Trinidad. Trinidadians did not pay any attention to it. The same thing happened when Marcus Garvey started his Universal Negro Improvement Association and African Communities League in Jamaica. He couldn't get it off the ground. The soil would not take the seed.

The soil was fertile, however, in the United States. And once you see this, you will understand that we must all look at the nature of our respective oppressors. The oppressor in the United States has taught us to face reality better than any of these other oppressors. The oppressors of the Caribbean and South America have taught them the illusion that one day they will join the club.

Our oppressor in the United States has taught us explicitly that you will never join the club. Even with what you call integration, another fakery, they still let you know that you can come in the club, but you will never be accepted. In this physical integration, in the Caribbean Islands and South America, if you're almost white a special place is made for you. Not in the house, but in the area close to the house. In the United States, if you've got one drop of one drop, our crude oppressor would place you with the blackest of the Blacks and at one word all of you would be placed in the same sack. So that's a reality. All those Whites have some advantage. The girls have some advantage in the domestic job market and the husband market. And another market which I will not mention. No place is made for them in their father's house[15]

Now back to Booker T.Washington and his school. When we look at the period between the speech (1895) and his mysterious death in 1915. During that twenty-year span this man stood astride the life of Black America in such a way that the social history of that period can be written around the life of this single man. He was, to say the least, a schizophrenic. Black Americans cannot afford to be only schizophrenic because we need more than two personalities. Even if they only have to deal with Black people.

I have gone only part of the way and I will begin to sum up my talk. But the main thing that I have to say is to point out where the Civil Rights Movement went wrong. These beautiful young people had not made the contact with the Civil Rights activists who had come before them, who went to jail and got their heads beaten at a time when there was no television, no radio, and no recording. And they made a great sacrifice.

I will conclude the talk with a quotation from a great African American woman poet mainly because we have gotten so involved in this white "lib" movement. It is not about us anyway. In the great civilizations of Africa, long before we knew Europeans existed, we resolved this question of the role of the female by making the female the first goddess in history and the first woman in history to ride at the head of their armies. The first female to challenge the foreigners. One challenged Octavius who became Caesar Augustus and one challenged Alexander of Macedon. There's a question of equality for women. We demonstrated that before the first Greek wore a sandal. We don't have to go through that again. This whole thing about equality is something for somebody else. We proved that once and then we got mixed up with these Westerners. But that's their problem.

In her poetry, Mari Evans has said that the solution is to "speak the truth to the people." She has repeatedly said and she has implied that if you give people the light, they will find their way.[16]

In the early poetry of Pauli Murray (later the Reverend Dr. Pauli Murray), in her *Dark Testament*, speaking of freedom, she says:

> Freedom is a thing like amber wine that
> luresman down a path of skulls
> For they killed the dreamer but not the
> dream, the dream is always the same
> The dream is about freedom.[17]

Professor Caroline Fowler of Atlanta University said (in speaking of the need to bring African people back together again):

> We need to look at each other more. We

need to get reacquainted with each other's personality. We need to remove the strangeness that has grown up between us across all the seas and all the centuries.[18]

In her classic poem, "For My People," Margaret Walker called for us to:

Let a new earth begin. Let a new race of men arise and take control.[19]

My answer to her is a collective answer. I say, Sister Margaret, we are men of vision and we see tomorrow, not as a male-dominated tomorrow. We see tomorrow as a collective tomorrow with males and females as equals. We say to her: We have heard the martial music. We accept the challenge. We are the new men. With our women at our side as equal partners in the enterprise of freedom, we are the new men, and we are prepared to take charge.

Chapter Seven

Unblemished, Uncorrupted Leadership

The following are excerpts from the keynote speech at the November 13, 1992 African International Forum in Harlem about Malcolm X and the Spike Lee movie, sponsored by the Patrice Lumumba Coalition

These are very critical times in our life as a people. Once more we are standing at the crossroads of history and I have a great feeling of dilemma that we are debating minor things and neglecting major subjects. I have not seen the film, and therefore I will have little to say about the film.

In my brief discussion with Spike Lee, I suggested that maybe the film should open when they threw the mangled body of Malcolm's father on the porch, and Malcolm as a kid, tugging at his mother's apron and asking, "What happened to father?" And his mother going slowly out of her mind.

That was the beginning of the making of the mind of Malcolm X because he began to deal with the contradiction in this nation. He had to go through a whole lot of other contradictions. People telling him what he could not be, the challenge within himself, and the question, "Why can't I be what other people are?"

I think one of the main reasons why at this juncture in history that a whole lot of phony people are gravitating toward that image, is that they sense something in Malcolm X that is needed not only by this people by all people. Unblemished, uncorrupted, uncompromised leadership.

We've had so many hustlers disguised as leaders, so many peddlers of people. We keep looking back at Malcolm and keep examining him over and over again. What was the lesson that he taught? He taught a lesson around a subject that impinges on our minds now, and we are confused about how to grapple with that subject. That subject is land and nation, because land is the basis of nation.

You can talk all you want about liberation. If you have no control over the land, you cannot solidify the nation. Zimbabwe is a good example. They came to pseudo independence with Whites controlling most of the land and most of the food supply. That's not independence. That's programmed dependence.

Now why the gravitation toward Malcolm X? Haven't we gone through a battery of leaders? Haven't we examined them and found them wanting? What we miss in looking at Malcolm X is how he related to the radical ministry of the past.

I knew Malcolm X from 1958, when we met, until two weeks before he was assassinated, and I talked with him consistently. I did not, even in the book that I compiled on Malcolm X, say very much about my relationship to him. So may phonies popped up after his death saying they were friends and pals of Malcolm X. I didn't want to be associated with these phonies. So I kept my relationship to myself. Most of it I have not written about to this day.

He was a man, one of the fastest learners that I have ever met in my life. You could give him information and he would read this information back to you, teaching you lessons over and above your instruction to him without offending you. He would speak to several audiences simultaneously using the same words without offending anyone in the audience. He could speak to the reader and the non-reader, the college professor and the illiterate, simultaneously, and his message would get across to all of them.

What then is the significance of Malcolm X for today? He called not only for the restoration of nationhood, womanhood, manhood, he called for us to restore to our historical memory the time when we were not dependent on other people to make decisions for us. When we were the masters of our destiny. He called on us to reconsider our position, not in the United States, but in the world.

The idea of an African American unity patterned after the Organization of African Unity started in the Saturday meetings after he broke with the Nation of Islam. He began to have these meetings at Old Flash Inn on McCombs Place in Harlem on Saturday morning when the cafe had no customers. Out of these meetings came the structure and the idea for the Muslim Mosque, Inc. and the Organization of Afro-American Unity.

The constitution of the OAAU was fashioned in my living room. Charles Kenyatta, still alive, was there. Lynn Chipplet, now living in California, was the secretary. My former wife was there. My mother-in-law, still alive, was there. So I'm not talking about ancient history or any kind of mystery. When we found matching phraseology in the Organization of African Unity, when we could approximate their words in developing the constitution for the Organization of African American Unity, he was as happy as a child.

And it is little known that Malcolm X, and this is what made him so devastatingly effective, he had a non-Muslim "cabinet" that fed him information but never told him what to do or how to do it. Yet we made sure that the information he dispensed was always correct. No one told him what to do with the facts but they made sure that the facts were straight.

The most memorable thing for me in this regard is one time when he wanted something on history, because I was in his history cabinet. His man picked up the folder at 7:00 A.M., he didn't get to read it until 9:00, and at 11:00 he debated four college professors on the Congo institution. He reduced them to crying children.

I gave him some newspaper clippings, some xeroxes of some work of Berrell including the book, *King Leopold's Congo*, and I gave him a small book, tantamount to a good-sized pamphlet, by Mark Twain, *King Leopold's Soliloquy*, that had a lot of statistics about murder of people in the Congo. I told him an old trick that I used to play often when I was active in the Left movement. When people are talking about something you don't know anything about, always switch the conversation to something you know about. Malcolm played that trick on those college professors, and they were begging for mercy. That was Malcolm. Sharp in mind, sharp in information.

I'm going to talk briefly about some neglected aspects of his life and some misinterpretations, some misconceptions about some of the things he did. I do not think we have studied his growth, his evolution very well. I do not think that we have put the right emphasis on how he came out of the mire.

I first met him in 1958. He came to look at the Nation of Islam's exhibit at the World Trade Show building, the African Heritage Exposition. He saw someone hanging around me, a Hungarian girl, and he kept looking, when she left, he came over and said, "That your woman?" I said, "No." He said, "Good. That's a dead-end street. I've been down that street." He went away, then came over again, looked me up and down and said, "I bet you're a pork eater./ I admitted that I visited the pork chop once in a while and that I had been known to admire and to enjoy some chitlins. He suspected it. Throughout all our relationship he kept razzing me about being a pork eater, a swine eater. He said, "You're a decent human being. I'm gonna give you 99. Leave that swine alone, I'll give you 100." I stopped eating pork about fifteen years ago. It had nothing to do with religion at all. It had something to do with health. I wanted to live a little longer and my high blood pressure just simply wouldn't take it.

Soon after this meeting he started a newspaper. He called it *Mr. Muhammad Speaks.* It later became *Muhammad Speaks.* And if you look at that first issue, if you're ever fortunate enough to get a rare thing like that, you'll find an article I wrote on the historical background of Nigeria. I told him how broke I was. I had recently married for the second time, and the job market wasn't going too good. I was working at night at a bank and editing a magazine that paid me the magnificent sum of about $70 a week. My wife was pregnant. Malcolm X paid me out of his own pocket, I found out years later. It wasn't the Nation's money, it was his own money.

You see, he began to pull around him people who could advise him on the fact of the evolution and change in our movement. He was interested in every aspect of that movement. On the eve of the March on Washington in 1963, he too was restless and asked for permission to participate in the march. Permission was not granted. This was part of the beginning of some difficulties (in the Nation of Islam). When it was discovered that Elijah Muhammad's health wasn't too good, certain jealous rivalries began to develop within the Fruit of Islam, and among some other people, who were thinking he would be the natural head of the Nation in the absence of Elijah Muhammad. Certain forces began to move against him within the Nation.

He had become the spokesman for the Nation. He had given the Nation a national presence. And many times, when he was prefacing his speech with the words "The Honorable Elijah Muhammad teaches us," he, Malcolm X, was teaching lessons over and above anything the Honorable Elijah Muhammad ever thought about. Yet he was crediting Elijah Muhammad for his words. Because in Elijah Muhammad, Malcolm X had found the lost father, the father that they (the Ku Klux Klan) had threw on that porch. He had again found a father image in his life and he loved and respected Elijah Muhammad like a father and tried to communicate with him up until within the week of his death, only to have his letters and his tapes intercepted. Elijah Muhammad would die without ever getting those last messages and that plea from Malcolm X for the two of them to get together and put that movement together again and heal the breach between them.

These are some of the things very few people know about, very few people write about.

Malcolm X knew the good that the Nation was doing, taking people out of prison, making them whole again, making them clean up themselves again, making them throw away old habits for new habits, teaching them respect for women again, teaching them responsibility again. The movement of Elijah Muhammad was not stealing people from the little church or the big church, because they weren't in there. These were the people out there with no appreciable rallying point, with no appreciable leadership, who had found basic leadership.

You have to understand the good of the Nation of Islam, whether you believe in Islam or not. That's not the issue I'm trying to get across here, because I don't believe in any form of organized religion. I believe in spirituality, and I believe in people. I believe in commitment. I believe in the worth of human beings. I believe in honor. I am an African nationalist and a Pan-Africanist. If you ever gave me a proper definition of Marxism that would fit within my Pan-Africanism and my African nationalism, I would be a Marxist. But if it takes me out of there, then you can have it because we had the same thing, without dogma, without formalization, before Europeans wore shoes or lived in houses that had a window. We didn't have to go to Europe for that kind of thing anyway, for that kind of society.

What I'm trying to get at is that on the eve of the March on Washington, when he was not given permission to participate in that big arena, although in the final analysis it was a picnic on the grass that achieved absolutely nothing. To him it was symbolic that the other organizations were going there, participating. He wanted the right to do the same thing. I think he would have had something meaningful to contribute to the March on Washington. It might have had substance with Malcolm X in it. Martin Luther King, Jr. had a dream. Malcolm X would have had a plan.

Soon after this, after the "chickens coming home to roost" statement , he was silenced. And it really wasn't this statement. They wanted an excuse to get him out anyway, so they used this flimsy excuse. When he saw that he wasn't going to be asked to come back into the Nation, he began to formulate ideas, organizational ideas, of his own. He began hurriedly, with such personnel and such support as he could get. Some were Muslims and some were non-Muslims. Some followed him out of the Nation, some rallied around him out of respect. But he was moving fast.

Now when we go to Africa, the trip to North Africa was not as significant as the rip to West Africa. And yet the trip to West Africa is basically left out of the Spike Lee movie, so I've been told.

There was an attempt to poison him in Egypt. This was no doubt because he did not know the warring factions within Islam in the name of Allah. There have always been warring factions within Islam, and still are, even now. He got trapped between these warring factions. Both of them wanted to control him.

When he went on the Hajj to Mecca and when he wrote back that he saw black Muslims, white Muslims, brown Muslims worshipping together, that was an observation, not an analysis. Too many people think this means he was now an integrationist. Soon after he arrived back here, he made clear he had not changed his ideas on race one iota, if you're trying to say that near the end of his life he became an integrationist.

Well, near the end of his life he met Martin Luther King, Jr.

King and Malcolm X had the same basic objective, walking down different roads using different methodologies. King's method would not succeed because he was appealing to the conscience of the oppressor, not knowing that the oppressor had no conscience. It was idealistic, but it was totally impractical. Malcolm X said in simple direct words again and again, "The oppressor has no conscience. The oppressor has not accepted your manhood or your womanhood."

I think the most unfortunate thing of the many unfortunate things that happened to Malcolm X is that a bunch of opportunists from the political Left gained control over his speeches. (This is a reference to Pathfinder Press and the Jack Barnes leadership team which influences it. Betty Shabazz, Malcolm's widow, gave Pathfinder exclusive rights to publish material by Malcolm.) They began to publish his speeches and interpret them, trying to prove that he was what they desired him to be.

Malcolm X is too big to fit into any kind of bowl. He's too big to fit into any bowl marked communism, socialism, or capitalism. He was a believer in the ultimate destiny of his people. Among his many revolutionary statements are the most important: "Ballot or the Bullet" and "Message to the Grassroots." In both of them he dealt with political power and the land question as the basis of the nation.

Some will argue about who assassinated him and why. But Malcolm X learned something on his way home from Africa, after he arrived in Paris and was barred from entering, after that he knew that the plan to destroy him was not designed by his own people. He knew that the apparatus was bigger than anything controlled by his own people. And he became somewhat fatalistic. He knew that master murderers were out to get him and no matter whose hand pulled the trigger, that was not the planning and design of Black people.

Once you show your people the true face of power and what to do about it in this country, one of three things is going to happen to you. You're gong to be driven into exile, driven into suicide, or you're gong to be assassinated. Once your people understand the true face of power and know what to do about it, someone's going to have to give them some power, or they're going to take it. Once he began to teach that lesson, he was writing his own obituary. The same thing is true of Martin Luther King, Jr. in his speeches on the war in Vietnam.

When Malcolm X was assassinated I was in Connecticut making a speech on great Africans in history. I was in the home of a Jewish family, having dinner before the speech. When they came in and told me, they were as cold as ice, and someone said, "After all, he was anti-Semitic." I didn't know what to say. I wanted to hit somebody. I wanted to kick and scream. I went into their bedroom and cried like a child for fifteen minutes. I came out, made a fast speech later that day, and went home.

But during that year after his death, after I had participated in the memorial for him, I often felt that I was having a conversation with an old friend. And near the end of that year, sitting alone in my downstairs office, with the conversation going again, I asked figuratively, "Malcolm, what can I do?" And I felt that somewhere someone said, "Do your best work." I knew then that my best work was part of what he lived for and part of the reason he died. To tell the truth and suffer the consequences, that was my best work.

Afterword

All of these speeches are about the African world position, one way or another. The 1950's marked a new era in African world relationships. The Africans in Africa were agitating for independence and demanding the fulfillment of promises made to them after World War II. Many Africans who, prior to this war, would have been put to death for lifting their hands against a white person prior to the colonial period, were now looking at the world from a different vantage point. Some were returning soldiers from World War II who had been trained to fight white Europeans other than their colonial masters. Some returned home with the idea of using their skill to fight against colonial oppression itself. Many missionary-trained Africans began to see the God that the missionaries had trained them to worship as having no respect for color. They began to question their status at home and abroad.

Agitation against colonial rule in Ghana led to the establishment of facsimile political associations that would later be developed into poolitical parties. The main political party in Ghana, the Convention Peoples Party (CPP), under the leadership of Kwame Nkrumah guided Ghana into independence in 1957. This spectacular action set Africa's political revolution in motion. After 1957 nations in Africa were coming into being almost weekly. By 1958 a conference of nine independent states in Africa was called by Kwame Nkrumah. Some of the ideas that came out of the Pan-African Conference in Manchester, England, in 1945, were becoming realities. A small West African nation, Ghana, under the political leadership of Kwame Nkrumah, began to take all Africa for a political walk in the sun. The African Revolution was born and growing fast. The independence fever swept over Africa and reinforced the aspirations of the Africans living abroad. The new leaders of Africa were men of vision who had challenged the right of foreigners to rule their respective countries. By the mid-1960's coups and countercoups and paid agents of the former colonial powers had frustrated most of the countries in Africa and stymied its promise. In the closing years of the 1980's a generation of Africans, some missionary-trained, and some educated abroad, had returned home, more Western than African. To put it crudely, most of these returning Africans were Europeans in black-faces who only superficially had Africa's interest at heart.

Because Africans had lost from their memory, the knowledge of how they ruled a state before the European and Arab interference, most of the states in Africa became imitations of European states. The nation-state, as designed by the Europeans, had not previously existed in Africa and worked against the cultural temperament of African people. Before the European encroachment and the Arab domination in North and East Africa, Africans lived in a cluster of territorial states of loose borders. The new nation-state was a betrayal of the Africa that existed before invaders, foreigners, fakers, and fools destroyed the structure of the states devised by Africans.

This tragedy in state formation is well examined in Basil Davidison's *The Black Man's Burden, Africa and the Curse of the Nation-State*. Africans had pseudo-independence in artificial states that were formed after 1957. They had what is often referred to as "flag independence," meaning independence with ceremony, without substance. In many ways, especially political and economical, these were still European colonies. Not a single state in Africa was based on African traditional values. Some of the customary courts still existed. Nearly all of the civil courts were based on European law or Islamic law in the Moslem-dominated states. Most of these new Africans, educated abroad, found difficulty in communicating with some of their own people. The living conditions of millions of Africans living in Africa changed very little with the coming of Independence. The new ruling class expressed too much interest in foreign cars, foreign ideas, and sometimes foreign women. In the new, hurriedly-erected universities, there were very few courses that dealt with African history in depth before the invasion of the Arabs and the Europeans. The African made the mistake of not properly looking back before looking forward. Very little interest was shown in the massive resistance movements that existed throughout the whole of the nineteenth century and well into the twentieth century. These movements set in motion the political alertness that made the independence explosion possible. This is the past that could have shaped the present and the future in Africa. Not knowing, the Africans' failure to understand this rich, revolutionary heritage in using the events and personalities that made it possible was tantamount to betrayal of the African political revolution that began to emerge after the independence of Ghana, 1957.

In their enthusiasm about the new states in Africa, most Africans forgot that the Europeans, and to some degree the Arabs, had no vested interest in the stability of these states. Wreck and ruin became the order of the day with opportunistic Africans stymieing the growth of their respective governments. The Organization of African Unity (OAU) and other organizations formed to create African solidarity looked good on paper but never became functioning realities.

It is too often forgotten that what is referred to as the African Revolution was not a parochial affair pertaining to Africans alone who lived in Africa. It was part of the revolution existing among African people of the world. In the Caribbean islands, especially Trinidad, where some of the most important ideas and plans for the unification of African people started, the colonial aftermath was not much different than in Africa. The idea of a Union of Caribbean States was a good conversational piece in conferences in London and sometimes in the Caribbean Islands. These conversations did not create a Caribbean Federation or an economic union of Caribbean states on the eve of independence or after. Caribbean people had, unfortunately, forgotten that the Pan-African idea was started by three Trinidadians: H. Sylvester Williams, C.L.R. James, and George Padmore. The Jamaican, Marcus Garvey, had used the concept of African unity to build the largest Black organization ever known: the Universal Negro Improvement Association (UNIA). This organization failed twice when Marcus Garvey tried to establish it in his homeland, Jamaica. It reached the peak of its success in the United States through Caribbean administration and massive African American support. Revolutionary ideas, in general, failed in the Caribbean Islands because their most fiery radicals and some of their greatest political thinkers were forced into exile. African Americans became the beneficiaries of this Caribbean tragedy. Hubert Harrison, who introduced Marcus Garvey to his first large American audience in 1917, found no appreciation for his talent in the Virgin Islands. His book, *When Africa Awakens*, is still worth reading as a revolutionary indictment of colonialism and worldwide oppression. This brain drain on Caribbean talent had started early in the nineteenth century. Edward Blyden of the Virgin Islands went to Liberia where he became president of Liberia College in 1881, and on two occasions Liberian ambassador to England. Caribbean scholars and radical activists played a major role in the early liberation movements in the United States.

The idea of a Caribbean Federation never advanced

beyond the talking stage. The new states in the Caribbean, including the non-English-speaking islands, were all poor imitations of European states. On a personal basis, thousands of Caribbean people began to ape the mannerisms of their former colonial masters. Prejudice based on shades of color created by their former colonial masters extended into the period of independence sometimes with more tragic repurcussions than before. Fascination for whiteness and a white value system crippled the possibilities of the development of a series of island-states based, at least in part, on remembered African values. European values and the color white became a crippling fascinating throughout most of the islands.

The revolution against slavery and for social change started in the United States early in the nineteenth century among a class of free Blacks and escaped slaves in the New England states and the Eastern seaboard. This aspect of the revolution produced men and women like Frederick Douglass, Henry Highland Garnet, Harriet Tubman, Sojourner Truth and many notable others. This group of free Blacks set in motion a lot of the agitation against slavery on the eve of the Civil War. After the Civil War a short-lived political revolution had some success until it was betrayed in 1884-85. In his book, *The Betrayal of the Negro*, Rayford Logan calls this period the "nadir" or darkest hour in Black America. Near the end of the nineteenth century a personality emerged who would stand astride the life of Black America in such a way, from 1895 until his death in 1915, that the social history of Black America for that period can be told mainly through our reaction to that one man and his activity. His name was Booker T. Washington. He was misunderstood in his lifetime and he is misunderstood now. He was a remarkably imaginative and creative institution-builder. He was a strategist whose strategy did not always work. Booker T. Washington and W.E.B. Du Bois had a difference of opinion regarding education and training that has been interpreted as a fight. It wasn't then nor is it now a matter of who was right and who was wrong. On careful examination it will be found that both of them were right. Du Bois was somewhat premature. We needed the educational and training ideas of Booker T. Washington then and now as much as we needed the political thinking of W.E.B. Du Bois. These two personalities guided Black America into the 20th century where a new aspect of the struggle for revolutionary change was set in motion. A high point of this revolution began to manifest itself after the Supreme Court decision in 1954 outlawing segregation in the schools. The Montgomery bus boycott, freedom rides, and sit-ins at lunch counters were a continuation of the same movement for upward mobility. The fight for equal pay for Black teachers was converted into a larger fight for equal education. The basis of what is referred to as the Civil Rights Movement was established. This movement reached its peak with the March on Washington in 1963.

In the mid-1960s many of the leaders of this movement were siphoned off by anti-poverty agencies and other activities. The Selma, Alabama, march and the continuous fight against second-class citizenship kept the greater part of the movement intact. Unfortunately, concurrent with the overthrow of the Nkrumah government in 1966, paid agents and out-and-out informers were destroying the effectiveness of what was referred to as the Black Revolution in the United States.

Stokely Carmichael's (aka Kwame Ture) call for Black Power was a stimulant to the movement. The call for Black Power produced no Black Power. It only produced the fear of its possibilities. The 1960s were the last flowering years of what is referred to as the Civil Rights Movement. In the '80s some of the participants wrote its epitaph. Many former participants found employment in the anti-poverty programs and other government-sponsored projects.

The glaring error during the aftermath of the Civil Rights

Movement was a misinterpretation of the word "integration." In retrospect, I think Black Americans should have asked for full justice as American citizens. Integration was one item in a large package and all of us should have had the prerogative to accept it or reject it. The right not to integrate was also a right that was worth serious consideration. Segregation itself and oppression in general had forced Blacks to build community institutions that were worthy of being preserved even when Blacks had access to other institutions. A large black student enrollment into previously predominantly all-white schools did not mean that the black schools needed to be deserted or rejected. One thing could have reinforced the other with some kind of complement. The traditional Black colleges were still needed now more than ever because more Blacks were now college-conscious. The Black community institutions should have grown stronger instead of being neglected into oblivion. The fact that Blacks could now go into white hotels did not mean that the small, well-kept hotels in many Black communities should have been abandoned. Most of these hotels were run by families and they were used by black musicians and entertainers and general visitors to the Black community. Many Blacks preferred these hotels because of the family hospitality in most of them and the well-prepared, traditional Black home cooking. Going into the white hotels, now open to Blacks, was an option. That option should not have been eliminated because of the lack of patronage. I have referred to the hotels as only one of the many useful accommodations in the Black community that declined and sometimes disappeared altogether with the coming of integration. Because we did not make selective and creative uses of integration, in the final analysis, it could have done the Black community more harm than good. This misunderstanding is part of the betrayal of the African American aspect of the African World Revolution. In the eyes of most Whites and the former colonial masters of Africa, the words "Black power" became a threat to their hold on the political and economic control of the African world. They assumed that this call for Black Power was also a call for Black statehood, true nationhood and black management of every aspect of their lives, including the rich mineral resources in Africa. They discovered that the call for Black Power and African unity was, in part, wishful thinking. A combination of forces of Africa's former colonial masters and international managers of the world's wealth systematically frustrated and bought off a large number of the leaders of the new African states, both in African and abroad. Blacks calling for Black Power did not train large numbers of Blacks in the proper handling of power. Because the heads of Black nations both in African and abroad were in most cases trained in Europe or in the United States, their method of handling power did not relate to the traditions of their people. These rulers became direct and indirect servants of the same power forces that once dominated their respective nations. To be the true handlers of power in a state, you must train people to handle everything in the state, from, the making of a pin that holds your baby's diaper together to the making of a locomotive. You must have well-trained and committed citizens who understand that a large number of them will not only have to fly an airplane, they will have to eventually make an airplane.

Before we shouted slogans like "Black Power" and "Nationtime," we should have made an inventory of every item that goes into a well-managed nation. And as a survival precaution, we should have had at least ten persons well-trained to take care of every joy category essential to the making and the maintenance for a nation. We shouted, "Black Power" too soon. We shouted "Nationtime" too soon. We were cavalier in the use of phrases like "Black and Beautiful." We should have known that the world is not run by blackness and beauty. It is run by power and those who know how to handle it properly and strategically. Being black and beautiful means nothing unless you are ultimately black and powerful. African people all over the world have been to long removed from the proper handling of state power. The best African societies and the best world societies were collective and communal. Unfortunately, the technique of how to handle a society of this nature has been lost from the historical memory of most African people. No state institution or society within the whole of the African world will ever be successfully run on a European model. In throwing off European dominance and pursuing state independence, Africans the world over should have reexamined all religious concepts and concepts of governance that they inherited from their former European rulers. All political, cultural, and religious institutions should have been reappraised and a concept should have been adopted relevant to the needs of African people and not the needs of their former colonial masters. The values of a traditional African way of life should have been reexamined and reconsidered.

Prior to interference by foreigners, fakers, and fools, African societies were based primarily on the structure of the family. In many ways, large African families had the structure of a miniature state with a built-in judicial system and customs that were stronger than law. Africans the world over should have stopped being consumers of foreign-made goods in favor of producing the things they wear, the food they eat, and being in absolute control of the institutions that educate their children. The main factor in the new education should have been to train African people to be once more completely in charge of the structure of the state. They should have learned how to process their mineral wealth and how to market it and how to use it as an instrument of international power. They should have begun this process by locating African people on the map of human geography. We should have rejected names forced on us by oppressors, such as "Negro," "nigger," and "native." While we were minorities in some countries, we were never a world minority. Between the African people in the Americas, the Caribbean islands, the islands of the Pacific, and in Africa itself, there are at least a billion African people on the face of the earth. First and foremost, African people need to make allies out of and among themselves. They should make other allies depending on their needs or do without allies when alliances cannot be made that are ultimately to our benefit. The economic system that enslaved and colonized African people the world over cannot save them. The basis of any African future must rest largely on our understanding of Pan-Africanism and African nationalism. Professor Willard Johnson of MIT has said, "African people can change the world if first they change themselves." This understanding is the main ingredient in the African World Revolution. This, indeed, is tomorrow's work. Africans who are in doubt about this work will say, "I will start it tomorrow." Africans who are sure of themselves will say, "I will start it today."

African history is as old as world history. In fact, African history is the essence of world history. In order to understand African history in its true light, it may be necessary to place Africa at the center of world history and to start the rest of human history from that center. With the second rise of Europe in the fifteenth and the sixteenth centuries and the creation of the slave trade and the colonial system that followed, the African people were systematically read out of world history. The Europeans knew then and now that you cannot successfully oppress a consciously historical people. They had to forget, or pretend to forget, all they had previously known about African people. They had to forget the meeting between Africans and what would become of the Europeans prior to the Greco-Roman period. They had to neglect that small body of significant literature on the role of the Africans in early Europe, in early Asia, and in early America. In order to justify the slave trade, the Europeans created an African people in their minds who never actually existed. They created a people with no known culture and no known contact with a civilized way of life. This was a lie then and it is a lie now. In the fifteenth and sixteenth centuries When Europeans began the process of the slave trade and eventually the colonization of most of the world, they not only colonized history, they colonized most of the information about history. The most tragic of all their colonizations was the colonization of image, especially the image of God. They showed little respect for the art, culture, and religion of the people they colonized. That was most of the world. Propoganda and mental colonization did for Europeans what armies could not have done.

When today one looks at the fight against Black Studies and the revival of history to reflect the contributions of non-European people to the cultures of the word, we are seeing the results of almost a thousand years of anti-human propaganda in favor of the Europeans. In most cases, they propagated a concept implying that the world waited in darkness for Europeans to bring the light. The truth is the contrary. Europeans destroyed more civilizations than they ever built. In most of the countries that they invaded, they did more harm than good. To see African history in its true light is to see human history in its true light, because so much of African history is the basis of human history. Of all the people in the world, the Africans are the greatest sufferers from the anti-history campaign launched by the Europeans. Their campaign literally reversed human history.

To do this successfully, Europeans had to ignore master-pieces in world history written by Europeans on ;the true history of Africa, especially Egypt. The African country the Greeks called Egypt had to be taken out of Africa altogether. The achievements of Egypt had to be assigned to some mysterious people who built the splendid civilization of Egypt and then disappeared. The Europeans forgot that the civilization of Egypt predates the existence of Europe. No non-African people would have entered Africa and built such a splendid civilization in African without first building a similar civilization at home. This rules out both the Europeans and the Asians of creating any durable civilization in Africa.

To acknowledge that the Africans were the creators of the splendor of Africa is also to acknowledge the Africans as thinkers, planners, and developers of great and imaginative ideas. In essence, this would mean to humanize the Africans. The Europeans dehumanized all Africans in their minds in order to justify the slavery system.

The fight to reclaim African history that started early in the nineteenth century over most of the African world was a search for definition, direction, and a search for Africa's place in the drama referred to as civilization. In the United States, this fight was started early in the nineteenth century by freed and escaped slaves in the northeastern states such as Frederick Douglass; William Wells Brown, the first Black novelist; the editors of Freedom's Journal, the first significant black newspaper; John B. Russwurm; and others. The tradition was continued by nationalist/activists like Martin R. Delany and Robert Campbell; and slave activists like David Walker, Gabriel Prosser, Denmark Vesey, and Nat Turner. These activists and black abolitionists were major factors in starting the agitation against slavery on the eve of the Civil War. Near the end of the nineteenth century, great personalities like Booker T. Washington and W.E.B. Du Bois emerged, advocating a new educational system, . Early in the twentieth century great nineteenth century activists like Frederick Douglass and Edward W. Blyden passed and left a legacy of the struggle for manhood. The fight for education early in the twentieth century after the passing of Booker T. Washington was led by women such as Mary McLeod Bethune, Nannie

Burroughts, Charlotte Hawkins Brown, and other female institution builders.

In 1915, Carter G. Woodson and other activists in Chicago founded the Association for the Study of Negro Life and history. They had benefited in part from a two-volume work written by George Washington Williams, *The History of the Negro Race in the United States*. From 1916 to his deportation in 1927, Marcus Garvey not only called attention to the need to reclaim our history but also the land of our birth. He built the largest black organization before or since. The concept of Pan-Africanism that had emerged early in the twentieth century expanded into a larger concept for a world union of African people by the middle for the twentieth century. Martin Luther King, Jr., the Civil Rights Movement in the United States, the concept of a Caribbean Federation, and the African Freedom Explosion climaxed in the first decade of the second half of the twentieth century. Agitation for a true definition of the role of African people in world history was a world-wide movement. Organizations like the American Society of African Culture, the International Society of African Culture in Paris, the Congress of Africanists, African Heritage Studies Association, the Association for the Study of Classical African Civilization (ASCAC), the Association for the Study of Afro-American Life and History, and the National Council for Black Studies (NCBC) were the main part of a national and an international effort to restore African history to its place as a part of world history. One of the many tangible results of this campaign was the planning for and completion of an eight-volume General History of African edited by Africans and other scholars with a positive attitude toward African people. The true light of African history was now like a flame, flickering in the wind and growing stronger than the wind attempting to extinguish it.

The argument over Nile Valley civilization and whether the country the Greeks called Egypt was a part of Africa still persists in spite of all the information new and old that proves that Egypt and Nile Valley civilization was an indigenous African creation. When Europeans first 'discovered' Egypt, they were in the process of enslaving other parts of Africa and they were headlong in their attempts to prove that this splendor, though in ruins, had no relationship to the rest of Africa. The Western academic community, in most cases, mortgaged their integrity in order to create the mythology of the non-African connection with Egypt. They could not then or now deal with the fact that Egypt was a composite nation and the culmination of a great number of civilizations created in Africa to the south. The Nile was the world's first great cultural highway. There has always been this large cadre of Europeans propagating the myth about the non-Africanness of Egypt. Another group of Europeans have documented their opposition to this view. Gerald Massey's six-volume work, *Egypt, Light of the World*, *Natural Genesis*, and the *Book of the Beginnings* are part of the older books on the subject.

Three German writers made an able contribution to the clarification of the status of Egypt in world history: A.H.L. Heeren's *Historical Researches into the Politics, Intercourse and Trade of the (Carthagenians), Ethiopians, and Egyptians*, published in 1835; Heinrich Barth's *Discoveries in North and in Central Africa* deals in part with the Southern African origins of Egypt; Leo Frobenius wrote a five-volume *History of African Civilizations* that was condensed into two volumes and published in English as the *Voice of Africa*.

Two issues of the *Journal of African Civilizations*, (are) worth rereading in regard to the subject of Egypt's role in African history. In the issue, *Nile Valley Civilization*, I call your attention to the article by Cheikh Anta Diop, "Africa's Contribution to World Civilization: The Exact Sciences." In the issue of this publication marked *Egypt Revisited*, I especially call your attention to Cheikh Anta Diop's article, "Origin of the Ancient Egyptians." In his book *African Origins of Civilization: Myth or Reality*, Cheikh Anta Diop expands his information on this subject. John Jackson and Chancellor Williams have written with great clarity on the subject. In Chancellor Williams' book, *The Destruction of Black Civilization*, I call your attention to his second chapter, "Egypt, Ethiopia's oldest Daughter."

The American disciple of Gerald Massey was Alvin Boyd Huhn. His books reflect the African origins of the world's religions. I especially call attention to *Who Is this King of Glory?*, which is in my opinion one of the best books written on the Christ story. In addition, *Shadow of the Third Century*, dealing in part with the African reaction to the conference at Nicea and *The Lost Christianity* dealing with some misconceptions about Christianity and its origins are also worth reading.

Black Man of the Nile and His Family, *The African Origins of Major Western Civilizations*, and *The African Origins of the Three Major Western Religions* by professor Yosef ben-Jochannan are most informative on this subject.

I have called attention to only a few of the many significant books on this subject.

Pan-Africanism and African Nationalism are too often misinterpreted as forms of Black Separatism, a move to organize Blacks against Whites. I think Pan-Africans might be understood if we also understood that for the last 500 years the world has been ruled in the main by White nationalism. In the fifteenth and sixteenth centuries, when Europe pulled out of the lethargy of the middle Ages and began to expand into the broader world, no nation in Europe was against this move. If there was an argument among Europeans at all, it was an argument over the spoils of conquest. Europeans' conquest and dominance over the land and commerce of most of the world was achieved by a form of Pan-Europeanism. Pan-Africanism was created as a means of relieving Africans of the burden of European dominance in order to create, at least symbolically, the concept of "One God, One Aim, One Destiny," as propagated by Marcus Garvey. The greatest contribution to the formal idea of Pan-Africanism was made by three Trinidadians: H. Sylvester Williams, C.L.R. James, and George Padmore.

The first Pan-African Congress was called in London by H. Sylvester Williams in 1900. W.E.B. Du Bois, who would later be referred to as "The Father of Pan-Africanism," was really the intellectual guardian of Pan-Africanism and its finest scholar. In my opinion, the first Pan-African Congress, 1900, and the fifth Pan-African Congress in Manchester, England, 1945, were the most significant. The basic ideas that went into the African independence explosion came out of the fifth Pan-African Congress convened by George Padmore, Kwame Nkrumah, and other Africans, some of whom would become future heads of state.

Again, in my opinion, what could have been the most significant Pan-African Congress and the first to meet on African soil was the sixth pan-African Congress. It was the largest and most diverse of these meetings, however it was unwieldy and very little was accomplished. Too many Africans from different parts of the world and from within Africa itself came with different agendas. Not much was achieved except some good and bad conversations and an unfortunate fight over ideologies, politically Left and Right. This should have been a preparatory meeting in order to clarify the terms on what the sixth Pan-African Congress should have been. The sixth Pan-African Congress that met in Tanzania, in my opinion, was a great opportunity misunderstood and killed by selfish, petty, amateur political hacks who had no clear idea of what the concept of

African unity could be.

If there is another Pan-African Congress, the representatives must be clear about the direction of the meeting. First, they must be clear about the meaning of the word, "Pan," which means "all." They will have to extend Pan-Africanism beyond its narrow concept to the idea of an African World Union.

What is being called Afrocentricity is a combination of the aftermath of the Civil Right movements, the African independence explosion, and the Black Studies Revolution. The propagators of Afrocentricity are merely asking for what most people of the world had all along and took for granted, that is, the right to look at themselves and the world around them through the lens of the culture and circumstances that produced them. When a people have been forced to look at themselves through the eyes of their oppressor, they long for the day when they can reverse this approach and look at themselves in a manner that makes them like themselves. The formal approach to what I would prefer to call Africancentricity started in the eighteenth century when the system of chattel slavery proved to be an unwieldy labor system and a move was made to use another system called colonialism, a more sophisticated form of slavery. This system, still restricted, permitted its subjects a glimmer of the light of hope. Some of them had access to reading, mainly the Bible, and when they could not see the image of themselves in a book that was supposed to be inspirited by God, they began to ask serious questions about how an entire people got lost from the respectful commentary of human history. Out of this period came 100 years of anti-colonial wars in Africa, massive slave revolts in the United States and the Caribbean islands, and the birth of a class of free Blacks and former slaves who became literate in their oppressor's language. Their first expressions were against slavery. Then they began to ask what had happened to Africa, the continent of their origins. Their minds rejected the idea that they were a people who had not produced art and literature. This reclaiming of self and this search for the place of African people in world history was the embryo of the concept now called Afrocentricity.

One of my criticisms of Afrocentricity is that its propagators are too narrow in whom they consider to be Afrocentrists. Martin Delany and the radical black ministry of the nineteenth century deserve some reconsideration in this regard. The early black woman poet, Frances Harper, needs reconsideration along with Harriet Tubman and Sojourner Truth. A literature reflecting the concept came out of this period, the first half of this century, in Africa, the Caribbean islands, and the United States. In my opinion the works of Edward W. Blyden in Liberia deserve reappraisal and reconsideration. In the latter half of the nineteenth century the picture is clearer after the emergence of W.E.B. Du Bois and his book, *The Suppression of the African Slave Trade to the United States*. His books, *The Souls of Black Folk* and *The Gift of Black Folks*, need to be studied as good Africancentric literature. His book *The Negro* (1915), the first survey of the African contribution to world history is told from an African point of view. Therefore, it is Africancentric literature. The two great journalists in the early nineteenth century, T. Thomas Fortune and William Monroe Trotter, were Africancentric in their dynamic editorial writings. Marcus Garvey, after 1916 until his deportation in 1927, would add new dimension to the concept. An examination of Alain Locke's anthology, *The New Negro*, would show that most of its contributors were Africancentric in their point of view, especially Arthur Schomburg's "The Negro Digs Up Past." This was the preface to what is now being called Afrocentricity. Figuratively speaking, the preface needs reconsideration before we start the book.

Before approaching education, I think the first thing we need to learn is the difference between education and training. Then we need to face another reality. Powerful people never give powerless people the kind of education they need that will threaten their power. Therefore, education for Blacks at the hands of Whites is somewhat a contradiction in terms. If we were educated instead of trained, we wouldn't be beholden to them and we would have enough power to deal with them as equals. Equality, like freedom, is something you take with your own hands. You protect it with your own hands. It is never left to you in a will and you cannot will it to the next generation. The next generation must also protect their education and their freedom with their own hands. In many ways true education is a form of freedom. African people the world over have mainly used the method of their oppressor or former oppressor to educate themselves. This is not education. This is training for dependency.

The major crisis facing African people the world over is that they have not been educated for the new reality. And the new reality is that African people must be educated to regain the main thing they lost during slavery and colonialism, the control of the state and their own destiny. We have been programmed into worshipping a god not of our own choosing and following a way of life alien to our tradition. Through the years I have repeatedly said education has but one purpose. Everything else is a waste of time. The main purpose of education is to train the student to be a proper handler of power. Every form of true education trains the student in self-reliance. When a student learns the difference between a red light and a green light, he or she is exercising control over his or her own safety. When you learn how to play a piano properly, you have power and control over sound. Education that fails to equip you to handle some form of power is irrelevant and not education at all.

African people need to stop shouting "nationtime" until they are clear about the responsibilities of running a nation. We need to stop shouting "Black Power" and learn that power has no color. Power favor(s) those who handle it properly and strategically. The first lesson is to learn to have power and control over yourself.

Before the recent film on the life of Malcolm X, writing about Malcolm X and speculating on where he would have gone before his life was ended was a small literary industry. Now, nearly thirty years after his death, a lot of people seem to be scratching at the grave of Malcolm X and asking for answers to questions that were both asked and answered during his lifetime. Malcolm X was both before and ahead, a man of his time. His life was an example of what a man can make of his life when he takes full charge of it. After seeing the movie on the life of Malcolm X, the opinion I expressed in the speech did not change one iota. The life of the person I knew wasn't in the movie at all. The movie maker seemed to have created a Malcolm that in his opinion was probably acceptable. In many ways Malcolm X was a continuation of the nineteenth century rebel black minister who, in the midst of the slavery period, called on slaves to take up arms against their slave masters. Malcolm X was not afraid to identify the enemies of his people and tell them how they should be dealt with. He was one of the truly great revolutionary leaders to appear in the United States in the twentieth century, black or white.

The movie about the life of Malcolm X is notable for what

it left out. No attention was paid to his African visits, his address to the organization of African Unity, and his personal conference with Kwame Nkrumah. The fact that Martin Luther King, Jr. and Malcolm X were coming close together on some issues was not emphasized in the movie. The remark about Martin Luther King, Jr., spoken by a white character in the movie, was not only poor taste, it was uncalled for. It was unnecessary and even vulgar. Malcolm X's lasting contribution to black revolutionary thinking was how he dealt with the land question. In his speech, "Message to the Grassroots," he emphasized that land is the basis of a nation. Of the rash of new books about Malcolm X, only a few of them are worth reading. Most of them say nothing new or revealing. In my opinion, the book, The Judas Factor, is the best of these new books. In the final analysis, my approach to Malcolm X is similar to my approach to the betrayal of the African World Revolution, because he was a part of the revolution. Two generations of Africans, both at home and abroad, failed to understand the true nature of the Africans' revolutionary mission. With Western education, they became Western imitators. Some of them became as corrupt as their former colonial masters. Most of the heads of African states accepted the wrong kind of framework for an African state. The European nation-state with its tight borders will never be affective in Africa. African cultures, and sometimes African people, are interchangeable between different areas.

Africans need the cultural cross-fertilization of relating to each other without border restrictions. After two generations of these traitors, it is my belief that there is a growing desire in Africa to put Africa back together again and make it function for Africans both at home and abroad. There is now a growing movement to adopt Pan-African nationalism as the essential connecting link between African people throughout the world. There are now some Africans ready to extend Pan-Africanism beyond its narrow base into an African World Community.

In my opinion, when this happens, the spirit of Kwame Nkrumah, George Padmore, and others who dreamt and planned the unification of Africa will be vindicated.

John Henrik Clarke
Professor Emeritus, African and World History
Hunter College, New York City
April 23, 1994

Notes

Chapter One:
WHO BETRAYED
THE AFRICAN WORLD REVOLUTION?

1. John Henrik Clarke, *Harlem, U.S.A.* (Berlin: Seven Seas Publishers, 1965). See also Adisa Makalani, ed., Black News Book Party for E. Curtis Alexander upon the publication of *Adam Clayton Powell, Jr.: A Black Power Political Educator*. Commentary by John Henrik Clarke, unpublished lecture notes recorded by Adisa Makalani on December 12, 1983, 4-5; Gilbert Osofsky, *Harlem: The Making of a Ghetto, 1890-1930* (New York/Evanston: Harper & Row, 1968); and Allon Schoener, ed., *Harlem On My Mind: Cultural Capitol of Black America* (New York: Random House, 1968).

2. Charles V. Hamilton, *The Political Biography of an American Dilemma* (New York: Macmillan Publishing Co., 1991). See also Roi Ottley, *New World A-Coming: Inside Black America* (New York: Ayer Co. Publishers, 1943, 1968); Gilbert Osofsky, *Harlem: The Making of a Ghetto* (New York/Evanston: Harper & Row, 1968); and John Henrik Clarke, *Harlem, U.S.A.* (Berlin: Seven Seas Press, 1965).

3. George Breitman, "Message to the Grass Roots." *Malcolm X Speaks: Selected Speeches & Statements* (New York: Grove Press, 1965), 7-17.

4. "Many of you know I have become interested in a concept called psycholinguistics. As you know June 'teenth is coming upon us. The key notion in June 'teenth is the Emancipation Proclamation.

"One of the things about the English language is that it is a plagiarist language for a 'few' years. They were communicating with wolves and going 'bow-wow.' They really don't have a long history of communicating when you go back and study this thing. If you go back and study English law you can't find a law book that goes past 900 years ago because the English could not communicate; they had no language. So they just really became a people who were capable of communication . . . they were barbarians.

"This word 'emancipation' . . . most of us take the position that this word means freedom . . . is that correct? I find that what you have to do with English . . . English is a subject that is deeper than making subjects and verbs agree. Yet, that is all you are taught in school. One of the things that you must do in terms of English is begin to find the root meaning of words.

"Emancipation is not an English term. It came from the Roman law and it means 'transfer of ownership.' Basically, what we're talking about here is that the Emancipation Proclamation did not free anybody because we always knew that Abe didn't free us. Am I right? Then the question becomes . . . if Abe Lincoln didn't free us, then who did? Certainly no Cracker did.

"This transfer of ownership' means that there was a recognition that the English model of slavery had to be changed and there had to be a Roman model of slavery. If you study Roman law, you'll find that the Roman system of slavery was different from the English system of slavery. In the Roman system of slavery you could be a banker, a lawyer, an architect, an engineer .. you could be any of that . . . just like we are today. You have Negroes who say, 'Yes, I graduated from Harvard University.' Yeah, a slave or . . . 'I'm Clarence Thomas' . . . a slave.

"We have to begin to understand that this whole thing was a question of double-speak. White folks knew from the beginning that emancipation had a meaning deeper than English. It was rooted in Roman language and based on the Roman experience. So as we go through June 'teenth we should really be very clear on what Emancipation Proclamation really means (Attorney Alton Maddox, *The Slave Theatre*, June 10, 1992)."

5. "Very often two cultures in Africa would meet and compliment each other without destroying either one. They would have the best elements from one put into the other without necessarily destroying any elements of either one. Their meeting embellishes the elements of culture and created a separate and distinct culture from the two that was better than either one by itself. Now that is the way Africans, and sometimes Asians leap culturally and diffuse the culture.

"A diffusion of culture differs from an amalgamation of culture and differs again from an annihilation of culture. A diffusion of culture is a wedding between cultures and they become one. Taking the best elements of both and sometimes letting each one exist to the compliment of each other. You have to look at the way the European looks at cultures. He looks at cultures that did not come form Europe as no culture at all. He will never acknowledge the equality of non-Western culture that is far superior to his; he goes back again to the drawing board . . . Mostly the history books try to prove that it wasn't non-Western at all. He will say that long ago, he came and discovered (created) this particular culture" (John Henrik Clarke, "African Contribution to Early World Culture, Chapter I," *African Contribution to World Culture*, Volume I (Harlem, NY: Publication Pending, October 9, 1984), 3-4; and Patrick Oster, "The Colonies Are Gone, But Not the Colonial View of Race," *Newsday*, September 23, 1992.

* Religion is the inner awareness of a factual dynamic relationship between the individual on one hand, and the cosmos and the world of nature on the other.

* Philosophy is the articulation of that relationship in a meaningful intelligible way, as a guide to a practical living.

* Drama is the enactment of that relationship in any medium whatever.

* Art is the meaningful expression of that relationship in any medium whatever.

* History is the factual record of that relationship in its process of becoming; not as mere statistical facts, but as the detailed diary of the contacts between man, cosmos and nature, from which were eventually distilled that clear awareness of the interdependence and the unbroken continuity between the three worlds.

* The science of social organization is an accurate reproduction of that same relationship, in terms of human society.

* The science of government is the codification of that relationship and its application in that society, its purpose being to subserve the science of social organization. Economics, family structure, and the individual within the family, are determined by, and subserve, the science of government and science of social organization (Chief Fela Sowande); see also Bill Cole, *John Coltrane* (New York, London: Schirmer Books, 1976), 21; and Fela Sowande, *Black Experience of Religion.* (Washington, DC: Howard University, 1970).

"We are into the African role in the rise of Judaism and

Christianity. There's nothing more cultural than a religion and there's nothing more political. If you think religions are about praying only, you have illusions. My main point is that religion is not only a part of culture, it is a part of the containment of culture.

"It is part of the rationale for culture existing and not only part, but sometimes the main rationale for power existing. I do not believe that religion should be taken solely from the point of power and culture. Religions taken in their purest form are generally practiced by the uninitiated and the uninformed politically and when they are not used on behalf of a nation, generally they are not effective in the defense of that nation. The moral basis for the defense of nations, their cultures, their power, and their politics exists in all religions. However, there is no defense in religion for the usurpation of other people's power, demeaning other people's cultures, and the destruction of other peoples. Yet most of the religions of the world have been used to do just that.

"Now what were the exceptions? Buddhism was never used as religion of conquest and was limited in its use as a religion of conversion. Buddhism was and still is a rather intellectual, esoteric religion that appeals to your intellectual reasoning as to why you should join it or not. If in your intellectual reasoning you decide not to join it, they just write you off as one of these people who happen to be knowledgeable enough, or bright enough to get the message . . . sorry for you.

"'We've shown you a good thing; you passed it up.' So you go on your way, but no fight . . . nobody's going to beat on you. Nobody's going to do anything to you except leave you alone in your ignorance of what a great religion needs to be.

"There are certain religions that relate in some way to Buddhism. Shintoism which is really the national religion of the Japanese relates to some extent to Buddhism. There are large numbers of Buddhists in Japan now. I want to show you before going back to the roots of these religions what religions have done for the world and the world's people.

"There are a whole lot of religions other than Christianity, Judaism and Islam. Although we're not going to talk about Islam in this chapter. The best known religions were very satisfactory to the people who practiced them and they saw no reason why they should be converted to other religions.

"In India, the religion of the Hindus seems sufficient for them. It has not changed a great deal from its original base. Their early god was similar to the Christian god; only it was Krishna, spelled with a 'k.' The people that you see dancing in the street singing 'Hare Krishna, hare Krishna,' are the Westerners who think they are practicing an Oriental religion.

"Oriental religions designed by Orientals generally don't fit the Western psyche. Many times they go into it and bring to it occultism that was not in the religion at all. Many times they go into Islam because there (is) not a large (number) of Whites in Islam.

"Turkey is basically an Islamic country, but there are probably just as many Christians there. Turkey is an Islamic-European country straddling between Europe and Western Asia. This explains why Christianity in Byzantium (Byzantine) had its headquarters in Turkey.

"The person who made Christianity the religion of the Holy Roman Empire, the Eastern Branch, later adopted by the other branch was from Turkey, Constantine. Constantine was from a city that was later to be called Constantinople, now called Ankara. The name was changed by the Turkish leader-liberator, Kemal Attaturk. In his attempt to modernize Turkey, he wanted to get rid of some of the old names.

"We're looking at religions that preceded Judaism; religions that laid the basis for what would later be called Judaism, Christianity, and Islam. These religions need to be reconsidered if not reconstructed. They were based on some things that are reasonable right now.

"I don't see anything wrong with making a deity out of Grand Papa and the ancestors who have gone on before. They are your messengers to the deity ... whoever that deity happens to be. The ancestor worship was very prevalent in African societies, sometimes in the Pacific and South Sea Island societies. It preceded Christianity but missionaries forcefully made Christianity more attractive in some ways and some of them joined it only to rule the day. Later on, the Royal Family in Hawaii, mostly black—which has been documented and proved—ruled in Hawaii, definitely had an African strain. The missionaries who wrote of the takeover said almost positively that these people were Black.

"There are other Black people practicing religions worship and sun worship. There was a group of people on an island near what is now Australia. The island is Tasmania. This is an incident in human history that a whole lot of people have forgotten and a whole lot of people didn't know in the first place. Here is an island where English prisoners and women of the evening came and destroyed every man, woman, and child. There's a book on it called *The Last Tasmanians*; these were Black people who met this fate. There's another book called *Black Australia* dealing with the destruction of the so-called Aborigines.

"Most people assume to call a person an Aborigine is insulting or downgrading, but Aborigine means you're the original; you're not a carbon copy. You're the original and this is the basis for people still to come. Let's look just a little more at this world, at the world before the advent of Judaism, Christianity, and Islam .. mainly before the advent of Judaism and Christianity. Here is a point where we need to consult very carefully Dr. ben-Jochannan's works: *The African Origins of the Major Western Religions* and *Africa: Mother of Western Civilization*. He is not saying anything new, nor does he pretend

---

that it is new. However, he is presenting it to a Black audience in a manner, hopefully, that they will understand. In looking at this presentation and then looking at concepts that would later develop . . . there is an arrogance in Christianity, Judaism, and Islam; it is an arrogance that is downright offensive.

"The arrogance is in the assumption that if you do not belong to them you are hopeless and there is no salvation for you. The assumption then is that all the people who lived and died before these religions came into being died without salvation. That's an insult. The assumption is that most of the world before these religions was wrong. Some of these religions are still being practiced; people are relaxed and successful with them. We also find that in today's Christianity a lot of Pagan rituals still exist.

"Recently in *The New York Times* there was an article about a Brazilian industrialist who engaged in Vodun (Voodoo) rites to make sure that the Vodun gods blessed him and gave him guidance for this big deal. Highly civilized, educated, college . . . all of that. Yet, in a country where African religions still influence European religions, many times men pray to God . . . but they don't forget Shango.

"These religions didn't die; some of them were integrated into the major world religions and laid the basis for the major world religions. The practitioners of these religions try to pretend that there was nothing there before they arrived. There was something there before they arrived that must be rescued for the good of the whole world. We must cut through some of this arrogance and look at these religions; but first we want to look at the world before Christianity and Islam (John Henrik Clarke, "The Twenty-Fifth Dynasty of Ancient Egyptian Culture, Chapter VIII," *African Contribution to World Culture*, Volume I (Harlem,NY: Publication Pending, November 27, 1984), 1."

6. "Nkrumah Founder of Modern Ghana," *Afrique Histoire*, Vol. 2, No. 1, 1984. See also J.B. Danquah, *The Akan Doctrine of God: A Fragment of Gold Coast Ethics and Religion.* (London: Frank Cass and Company Ltd, 1944, 1968).

7. J.A. Rogers, "Mohammed Ahmed, The Madhi," *World's Great Men of Color*, Volume I (New York: Macmillan Publishing, 1946, 1972), 295-309.

Fuzzy-Wuzzy
(Soudan Expeditionary Force)

We've fought with many men acrost the seas,
An' some of 'em was brave an' some was not:
The Paythan an' the Zulu an' Burmese;
But Fuzzy was the finest of the lot.
We never got a ha'porth's change of 'im
'E cut our sentries up Suakim,
An' 'e played the cat an' banjo with our forces,

So 'ere's to you, Fuzzy-Wuzzy, at your 'ome in the Soudan;
You're a poor benighted 'eathen but a first class fighten' man;
We gives you your certificate, an' if you want it signed
We'll come and an 'ave a romp with you whenever you're inclined.
We took our chanst among the Kyber 'ills,
The Boers knocked us silly at a mile,
The Burman give us Irriwaddy chills,
An' a Zulu impi dished up in style:
But all we ever got from such as they
Was pop to what the Fuzzy made us swaller;
We held our bloomin' own, the paper say,
But man for man the Fuzzy knocked us 'oller.

Then's 'ere's to you, Fuzzy-Wuzzy, an' the missis and the kid;

Our orders was to break you, an' of course we
went an' did.
We sloshed you with Martinis, an' it wasn't 'ardly
fair;
But for all the odds agin' you, Fuzz-Wuz, you
broke the square.
'E 'asn't got no papers of 'is own,
'E 'asn't got no meals nor rewards,
So we must certify the skill 'e's shown
In usin' of 'is long two-'anded swords:
When 'e's 'oppin' in an' out among the bush
With 'is coffin-'eded shield an' shovel-spear,
An 'appy day with Fuzzy on the rush
Will last an 'ealthy Tommy for a year.

So 'ere's to you, Fuzzy-Wuzzy, an' your friends
which are no more,
If we 'adn't lost some messmates we would 'elp
you deplore;
But give an' take's the gospel, an' we'll call the
bargain fair,
For if you 'ave lost more than us, you crumpled
us the square!

'E rushes at the smoke when we let drive,
An' before we know, 'e's 'ackin at our 'ead;
'E's all 'ot sand an' ginger when alive,
An' 'e's generally shammin' when 'e's dead.
'E's a daisy, 'e's a ducky, 'e's a lamb!
'E's a injia-rubber idiot on the spree,
'E's the on'y thing that doesn't give a damn
For a Regiment of British Infantree!

So 'ere's to you, Fuzz-Wuzzy, at your 'ome in the
Soudan;
You're a pore benighted 'eathen but a first-class
fightin' man;
An' 'ere's to you, Fuzzy-Wuzzy, with your 'ayrick
'ead of 'air
You big black boundin' beggar—for you broke
a British square.
(*Collected Verse of Rudyard Kipling*, "Fuzzy-

Wuzzy [Soudan Expeditionary Force]" (New York: Doubleday, Page & Co, 1910), 279-280.

8. J.A. Rogers, "Mohammed Abdullah (Mad Mullah)," *World's Great Men of Color*, Volume II (New York: Macmillan Publishing Company, 1947, 1972), 543.

9. John Henrik Clarke, *The Lives of Great African Chiefs* (Pittsburgh: Pittsburgh Courier Publishing, ND). See also Winston Churchill, *The River War* (London: Eyre and Spottisdwoode, 1899, 1951).

10. Eric Williams, *From Columbus to Castro: A History of the Caribbean* (New York: Vintage, 1984). See also Yusef A. Salaam, *Capoeira, African Brazilian Karate* (Harlem: Self Published, 1983); Jan Gabriel Steadman, *Narrative of a Five Years' Expedition, Against the Revolted Negroes of Surinam . . . from the year 1771, to 1777* (London: J. Johnson and J. Edwards, ND); and John Henrik Clarke, "The Origins of Current Afrikan Consciousness" (Harlem, NY: Unpublished Lecture, 1985).

11. George Padmore, *Africa and World Peace* (London: Frank Cass and Co, Ltd, 1937, 1972). See also George Padmore, *Pan-Africanism, or Communism?* (Garden City, NY: Anchor Books, 1972); and P. Olismanwuche Esedebe, *Pan-Africanism: The Idea and Movement, 1776-1963* (Washington, D.C: Howard University Press, 1982).

12. Hollis R. Lynch, *Edward Wilmot Blyden: Pan-Negro Patriot, 1832-1912* (London/Oxford: Oxford University Press, 1967). See also John G. Jackson, *Hubert Henry Harrison: The Black Socrates.* (Austin, TX: American Atheist Press, 1987); C.L.R. James, *History of Pan-African Revolt* (Washington, D.C: Drum and Spear Press, 1969); J.A. Rogers, "Edward Wilmot Blyden: Linguist, Educator, Statesman and African Patriot," *World's Great*

Men of Color, Volume II (New York: Macmillan Publishing Co., Inc., 1947, 1972), 294-297; J.A. Rogers, "Marcus Garvey: Provisional President of Africa and Messiah," *World's Great Men of Color,* Volume II (New York: Macmillan Publishing Co., Inc., 1947, 1972), 415-431; and J.A. Rogers, "Hubert Henry Harrison: Intellectual Giant and Freelance Educator," *World's Great Men of Color,* Volume II (New York: Macmillan Publishing Co., Inc., 1947, 1972), 432-447.

13. Amy Jacques Garvey, *Philosophy and Opinions of Marcus Garvey.* (New York: Atheneum, 1923, 1968). See also Amy Jacques Garvey, *Garvey and Garveyism* (New York: Macmillan Publishing Co., Inc., 1963, 1968); John Henrik Clarke, ed. with Amy Jacques Garvey, *Marcus Garvey and the Vision of Africa* (New York: Random House, 1973); Tony Martin, *Race First: The Ideological and Organizational Struggles of Marcus Garvey and the Universal Negro* (Westport, CT: Greenwood Press, 1976); Tony Martin, *Marcus Garvey, Hero* (Dover, MA: Majority Press, 1983); Tony Martin, *Literary Garveyism* (Dover, MA: Majority Press, 1983); Tony Martin, *The Pan-African Connection, From Slavery to Garvey and Beyond* (Dover, MA: Majority Press, 1983); George Padmore, *Pan-Africanism or Communism?* (Garden City, NY: Anchor/Doubleday, 1972); and P. Olisanwuche Esedebe, *Pan-Africanism: The Idea and Movement 1776-1963* (Washington, D.C.: Howard University Press, 1982).

14. Lerone Bennett, "Nay-Sayer of the Black Revolt: Henry Highland Garnett," *Pioneers in Protest* (Chicago: Johnson Publishing Company, 1968), 149-158. See also Lerone Bennett, "Father of the Protest Movement: Frederick Douglass," *Pioneers in Protest* (Chicago: Johnson Publishing Co., 1968), 197-217; John H. Bracey, Jr., August Meier, and Elliot Rudwick, eds., *Black Nationalism in America* (Indianapolis: Bobbs-Merrill Educational Publishing, 1970); Philip S. Foner, ed., *The Voice of Black America.*

Volume I: "Major Speeches by Blacks in the United States, 1979-1900" (New York: Capricorn Books, 1972, 1975); Vincent Harding, *There Is A River, The Black Struggle for Freedom in America* (New York: Harcourt Brace Jovanovich, 1981); and Gary Willis, "Lincoln's Black Theology," *Under God: Religion and American Politics* (New York: Simon and Schuster, 1990), 207-221.

15. Rayford W. Logan, *The Betrayal of the Negro: From Rutherford B. Hayes to Woodrow Wilson* (London: Collier-Macmillan, Ltd, 1954, 1965). See also W.E.B. DuBois, *Black Reconstruction in America, 1860-1880* (New York: Atheneum, 1935, 1962, 1969).

16. "We have to realize that education has but one honorable purpose ... one alone ... everything else is a waste of time: that is to train the student to be a proper handler of power. Being black and beautiful means nothing unless ultimately you're Black and powerful. The world is ruled by power, not blackness and beauty.

"If the day comes when fate is so cruel that it will let the meek inherit the earth ... the strong are going to inherit the meek and the status quo is going to remain the same. And powerful people never educate powerless people in what they need that they can use to take the power away from powerful people; it's too much to expect. If I was in power I would not educate people in how to take my power away from me" (John Henrik Clarke, "Columbus," *Like It Is* [WABC Public Affairs Television], [New York: Capitol Cities Broadcasting, taped: July 2, 1992, airdate: July 12, 1992]. Transcript available from Journal Graphics: Denver, CO).

"Those who profess to favor freedom yet deprecate agitation are men who want crops without plowing up the ground; they want rain without thunder and lighting. They want the ocean without the awful roar of its many waters.

"This struggle may be a moral one, or it may be a physical one, and it may be both moral and physical, but it must be a struggle. *Power concedes nothing without a demand. It never did and it never will. Find out just what any people will quietly submit to and you have found out the exact measure of injustice and wrong which will be imposed upon them, and these will continue till they are resisted with either words or blows, or with both. The limits of tyrants are prescribed by the endurance of those whom they oppress.*

"... Men may not get all they pay for in this world, but they certainly must pay for all they get. If we ever get free from the oppression and wrongs heaped upon us, we must pay for their removal. We must do this by labor, by suffering, by sacrifice, and if needs be, by our lives and the lives of others" (Frederick Douglass, "West India Emancipation (1857)," speech delivered in Canandaigua, NY, in Philip S. Foner, ed, *The Life and Writings of Frederick Douglass.* Volume II: "Pre-civil War Decade, 1850-1860" (New York: International Publishers, 1950), 437. Emphasis added).

17. Casely Hayford, *The Truth about the West African Land Question* (New York: Negro Universities Press, 1969). See also Jomo Kenyatta, *Kenya; Land of Conflict* (19).

18. Shawna Maglangbayan, "The Aryan Offensive Against Lumumba," *Garvey, Lumumba, Malcolm: Black Nationalist Separatists* (Chicago: Third World Press, 1973, 1976, 1979), 48-64.

19. "Road to Brown: The Biography of Charles Hamilton Houston." Video presented on Pubic Television (PBS) January 1991.

20. Malcolm X, "Message to the Grassroots," *Malcolm X Speaks* (New York: Grove Press, Inc, ND), 14-17.

21. T. Albert Marryshow, *Cycles of Civilization* (1922).

22. Clayborne Carson, *In Struggle: SNCC and the Black Awakening of the 1960's* (Cambridge, MA/London: Harvard University Press, 1981).

23. Paul Lewis, "Food Production and the Birth Rate Are in a New Race," *The New York Times*, May 10, 1992).

"Gastronomic delights are tickling tastebuds in French schools as part of the curriculum. Some 6,000 primary-school children in Paris have started taking a pilot program designed to encourage a taste of home-grown cuisine rather than American-style fast food.

"France has developed an art of living which we all need to rediscover and to safeguard,' said Culture Minister Jack Lang, who has attacked the American invasion of traditional French eating habits (Reuters, "French Fried About Kids' Fast Food Habits," *Newsday*, February 5, 1992).

"Top Japanese government and ruling party officials agreed yesterday that Japan should do all it could to meet U.S. demands for steps to redress the huge trade imbalance between the two nations. But they remained adamant in opposing any opening of Japan's rice market to imports" (Wire Service, "Japan Firm on Rice," *Newsday*, December 27, 1991).

"In the spring of 1968, a shot rang out in Memphis. In the same spring, thousands of shots rang out in Song My and My Lai and throughout scores of villages in South Vietnam, striking down hungry men, women, children, babies. It was as though the shots of Memphis and my Lai were fired from the same round. The shots did little to destroy the hunger; they killed the hungry, instead.

"In Memphis and in Song My, it was the same war.

"There are other ways to kill a people or colonize them, but none is more effective than the denial or control of their food. This is true whether the colony is in South Carolina or in South Korea. Indeed, you are what you eat: if you eat nothing, you soon are nothing. Hunger kills.

"Mrs. Fannie Lou Hamer, the brave Black civil rights lady of Ruleville, Mississippi, still ailing and lame from police beatings over the years, was resting on a bench in the lobby of the Sheraton-Park Hotel (which was hosting a White House Conference on Food and Nutrition). Asked whether she would favor such birth control measures as those proposed by Dr. Lowe's panel, she responded with shock and grave disappointment. "What?!' she exclaimed. "What are you talking about? Birth control? I didn't come here to talk about birth control. I came here to get some food to feed poor, hungry people. Where are they carrying on that kind of talk?

"Hearing the location, and without another word, the gallant lady pulled herself up on a cane and headed for the panel's meeting room. Along the way, she spotted certain Black men whom she summoned to follow her. She arrived at the room with about half a dozen bold Black men who walked to the front of the room and stood like soldiers. Mrs. Hamer followed them to the front and stood in the center of the panel leaders, demanding to be heard. Dr. Lowe yielded.

"She then demanded that the birth control proposal, which had just been adopted be reconsidered. After a ten minute oration, spelling out the horror of such a law in the hands of public officials she had known, the resolution was obliterated. After a promise from Dr. Lowe and the panelists that no such resolution would be further entertained, Mrs. Hamer and her Black male aids marched out as directly as they had come.

"Quite apparently, a major objective of what was originally called 'The White House Conference on Hunger' had failed.

However, that tentative failure by no means obscured from the poor a clear attitude which the government would seek to implement as law and policy: The solution to the hunger problem would not be more food to feed the hungry, but fewer hungry persons to be fed (Samuel F. Yette, *The Choice: The Issue of Black Survival in America* (New York: Berkeley Medallion Books, 1972), 100-101; 115-116.

"If China can feed a billion people, do you mean Africa can't feed half that many? Lately because the isolation of China never permitted outsiders to takeover China very much. But the basic feeding culture . . .and hear me well . . . If someone else takes over your feeding culture they decide life or death. No one ever took over the feeding culture of China, therefore they can use a combination of old ways and the new ways and they can innovate" (John Henrik Clarke, "The Two Golden Ages, Chapter IV," *African Contribution to World Culture*, Volume I (Harlem, NY: Publication Pending, October 20, 1984), 10-11)."

Chapter Two:
THE TRUE LIGHT OF AFRICAN HISTORY

1. *Unity in Action: A Photographic History of the African National Congress, South Africa: 1912-1982* (London: African National Congress, 1982).

2. V.T. Rajshekar, *Dalit: The Black Untouchables of India* (Atlanta/Ottawa: Clarity Press, 1987).

3. "Rebels Against the Raj: Nationalists and British Rule in India." Program produced by *Intercom* (Public Broadcasting Company). Professor Leonard Gordon of City University of New York provides the commentary, June 12, 1990. Information is on

videotape.

4. "You must learn to make jobs for yourselve so that the next time the boss tells you he does not have any work for you, you can tell him that you are going to do some work for yourself" (The Honorable Elijah Muhammad). See also G.K. Osei, *The Immortal Words of Great Africans* (London, England: The African Publication Society, 1980), 51.

5. "It is no doubt flattering to our vanity to imagine that the peoples of Africa were "primitive" and "barbarous" before the penetration of the Europeans, and that it was we who "civilized" them. But it is a theory that lacks historical foundation. The Empire of Ghana flourished in what is now French West Africa during the Dark Ages of Western Europe. By the fifteenth century there were Universities at Timbuktu (actually the University (of Sankore) was established earlier). The Ashanti of the Gold Coast and the Yorubas of Nigeria possessed highly organized and complex civilizations long before their territories were brought under British political control. The thesis that Africa is what Western European missionaries, traders, technicians, and administrators have made it is comforting (to Western Europeans) but invalid. The eruption of Western European colonizers into Africa with all the effects of their religion and schools, their gin and their cotton goods and their systems of administration is only an event, though a very important event, in the history of African people.

"If therefore, we wish to understand the national movements that have emerged in Africa we have to begin by trying to rid our minds of the European preconceptions that influence our thinking on this subject. This is not easy, since most of the available material on African affairs is presented from a European standpoint either by imperial historians who are interested in the record of European penetrations into Africa, or by colonial administrators (who are interested in the pattern of instructions imposed by European governments upon African societies) or by anthropologists who are often, though not always, mainly interested in the forms of social organizations surviving in the simplest African communities, considered in isolation from political developments in the world around them. We shall probably have to wait a little while for the real history of Africa to be written by African scholars for an African reading public" (Thomas Hodgkins, *The Highwayman* (1953). Emphasis added).

6. I.A. Akinjogbin, *History and Nation Building* (Ife, Nigeria: University of Ife Press, 1978). See also Edward Wilmot Blyden, *The Aims and Methods of a Liberal Education for Africans* (New York: George Young, 1882, 1920); and Edward Wilmot Blyden, *African Life and Customs* reprinted from *The Sierra Leone Weekly News* (London: C.M. Phillips, 1908).

"There is unity, equality, and at the same time priority or paramountcy all the groups together composing the social system. Self-government is exercised always with the family group and there is also within every group recognized and acted upon this general principle, that the efforts of all are and must be made for the good of each and the good of all.

"Under the African system also no stealing takes place. The necessity and the habit of theft do not arise, because everybody had his rights, and everybody has enough" (Edward Wilmot Blyden in G.K. Osei, *The Immortal Words of Great Africans* (London: The African Publication Society, 1980) 15-16).

7. "I think the whole method of educating people is such that we are taught to turn away from our own system. The most important education from what I can see is the informal education within the community, within the family, within the local

society . . . not in the school. The school can teach you how to read and write and so on; but it's not going to teach the whole liberation concept from our point of view (John Henrik Clarke, "Chapter Seven: Afrikan Culture as a Factor in the Resistance to Slavery in the Eighteenth Century," Richard Williams is the speaker, *Harlem School for Afrikana Studies: African Dimensions of World Culture*, Part II (Harlem, NY: Publication Pending, May 27, 1986), 25)."

"The assumption was also that there was no moral law in the world before Christianity (and that is not so). When you study some of the Pagans, there moral law holds up very substantially with that of the Christians" (John Henrik Clarke, "Chapter Seven: Afrikan Culture as a Factor in the Resistance to Slavery in the Eighteenth Century," *Harlem School for Afrikana Studies: African Dimensions of World Culture*, Part II (Harlem, NY: Publication Pending, May 27, 1986), 13).

8. "The compound is a civilization within itself. While I was there I saw an Englishwoman. She was writing a book on the Akan, she's probably an authority now. . . wherever she is. She came at 10:00 a.m. and left at 3:00 p.m. She missed the whole thing. You will never understand the civilization of a people you haven't had breakfast with. The father of breakfast gives the instruction and the advice for the day. He finds out who is going to do what before he goes over into town, but after 3:00 p.m. he's coming back. Then the last meal of the day, more talk, more instruction (John Henrik Clarke, "Chapter Three: The Nile Valley and its Contributions to the World," *Harlem School for Afrikana Studies: African Contribution to World Culture*, Part I (Harlem, NY: Publication Pending. October 23, 1984), 10)."

9. " . . . in 800 A.D., a wise Ethiopian named Abi Har pulled the Ethiopian Christians out of the Egyptian Coptic Church and

denied the Egyptians access to the Ethiopian Coptic Church. The Abun (the head or the Pope of the Church) used to come from Egypt. Abi Har stopped that.

"Now the Abuna of the Ethiopian Church had to come from Ethiopia because he assumed that those Copts were so corrupt and so involved in the Mediterranean, Eastern, and European politics that they did not understand indigenous African religions. It was a wise move and it's a move we need to study" (John Henrik Clarke, "Chapter One: African Contribution to Early World Culture," *Harlem School for Afrikana Studies: African Dimensions of World Culture*, Part I (Harlem, NY: Publication Pending, October 9, 1984), 21-22). See also John G. Jackson, "Ethiopia and the Origin of Civilization," *Introduction to African Civilizations* (Secaucus, NJ: The Citadel Press, 1970, 1980), 60-92)."

10. Graham Hancock, *The Sign and the Seal: The Quest for the Lost Ark of the Covenant* (New York: Crown Publishers, Inc., 1992).

11. J.A. Rogers, "Akhenaton: The First Messiah and Most Remarkable of the Pharaohs," *World's Great Men of Color*, Volume I (New York: Macmillian Publishing Company, 1946, 1972), 56-66.

12. "The coloured races are highly susceptible of religion; it is a constituent principle of their nature, and an excellent trait in their character. But unfortunately for them, they carry it too far. Their hope is largely developed, and consequently, they usually stand still, hope in God, and really expect Him to do that for them, which it is necessary they should do for themselves (Martin R. Delany. See also G.K. Osei, *The Immortal Words of Great Africans*. (London: The African Publication Society, 1980), 22).

13. G.K. Osei, *The Immortal Words of Great Africans* (London: The African Publication Society, 1980), 11.

14. Herbert Aptheker, *A Documentary History of the Negro People in the United States*, Three Volumes (Secaucus, NJ: Citadel Press, 1954-1974). See also Lerone Bennett, *Pioneers in Protest* (Chicago: Johnson Publishing Co, 1968); John H. Bracey, Jr., August Meier, and Elliot Rudwick, *Black Nationalism in America* (Indianapolis: Bobbs-Merrill Educational Publishing, 1970); and Benjamin Brawley, *Negro Builders and Heroes* (Chapel Hill: University of North Carolina Press, 1937); Iva E. Carruthers, *Bishop Henry McNeil Turner: A Biographical Sketch* (Chicago: Maat Publishers, 1977); John Henrik Clarke, "Chapter Eight: the Diffusion of Afrikan And European Culture in the Nineteenth Century," *Harlem School for Afrikana Studies: African Dimensions of World Culture*, Part II (Harlem, NY: Publication Pending, May 27, 1986); Anna Julia Cooper, *A Voice from the South* (New York/Oxford University Press, 1892, 1988); Philip S. Foner, ed, *The Voice of Black America: Major Speeches by Blacks in the United States 1797-1973*, Volume I (New York: Capricorn Books, 1972); Paula Giddings, *When and Where I Enter: The Impact of Black Women on Race and Sex in America* (New York, NY: William Morrow and Co, 1984); Vincent Harding, *There is a River, the Black Struggle for Freedom in America* (New York/London: Harcourt Brace Jovanovich, 1981); William Loren Katz, *The Black West: A Documentary and Pictorial History* (Garden City, NY: Doubleday/Anchor Books, 1971, 1973); Elie Kedourie, "The Negro in Ancient History" by Edward Wilmot Blyden (1871) in *Nationalism in Asia and Africa* (New York: New American Literary, 1970), 250-274; Hollis R. Lynch, *Edward Wilmot Blyden: Pan-Negro Patriot, 1832-1912* (London/Oxford/ New York: Oxford University Press, 1967, 1970); Marcia A. Matthews, *Richard Allen* (Baltimore/Dublinn: Helicon Press/ Helicon Ltd, 1963); Edwin S. Redkey, *Black Exodus: Black*

Nationalist and Back-to-Africa Movements, 1890-1910 (New Haven/London: Yale Univeristy Press, 1969); J.A. Rogers, *World's Great Men of Color*, Volume II (New York: Collier Books, 1947, 1972); Milton C. Sernett, "Chaper Two: Slave Religion in the Antebellum South," *Afro-American Religious History: A Documentary Witness* (Durham, NC: Duke University Press, 1985), 63-132; Milton C. Sernett, "Chapter Three: Black Churches North of Slavery and the Freedom Struggle," *Afro-American Religious History: A Documentary Witness* (Durham, NC: Duke Univeisty Press, (1985), 135-226; Milton C. Sernett, (Chapter Four: Freedom's Time of Trial: 1865-World War I," *Afro-American Religious History: A Documentary Witness* (Durham, NC: Duke University Press, 1985), 229-305; Booker T. Washington, *Up From Slavery* (New York: Penguin Books, 1900, 1986); and Booker T. Washington, *The Story of My Life and Work* (Toronto/Napierville, IL/Atlanta: J.L. Nichols & Co, 1900).

15. Herbert Aptheker, *American Negro Slave Revolts* (New York: International Pulbishers, 1943, 1963). See also Herbert Aptheker, *Nat Turner's Slave Rebellion* (New York: Humanities Press, 1966); Lerone Bennett, "Fanon of the Nineteenth Century: David Walker" and "A Burning for a Burning: Nat Turner," *Pioneers in Protest* (Chicago: Johnson Publishing Co, 1968), 67-97; and Vincent Harding, "Symptoms of Liberty and Blackhead Signposts: Daniel Walker and Nat Turner," *There is a River, The Black Struggle for Freedom in America* (New York: Harcourt Brace Javonich, 1981).

16. C.L.R. James, *The Black Jacobins: Toussaint L'Ouverture and the San Domingo Revolution* (New York: Vintage Books, 1963). See also Eric Williams, *From Columbus to Castro: The History of the Caribbean* (New York: Vintage Books, 1970).

17. W.E.B. Du Bois, *Souls of Black Folk.* (New York: New

American Library, 1903, 1969, 1982). See also W.E.B. Du Bois, *The Gift of Black Folk: Negroes in the Making of America* (Boston: The Stratford Co., 1924).

18. W.E.B. Du Bois, *Black Reconstruction in America, 1860-1880* (New York: Harcourt, Brace, 1935). See also Rayford W. Logan, *The Betrayal of the Negro, From Rutherford B. Hayes to Woodrow Wilson* (London: Collier-Macmillan, (1954).

19. Lerone Bennett, "Father of the Protest Movement: Frederick Douglass," *Pioneers in Protest* (Chicago: Johnson Puboishing Co., 1968), 195-217. See also Martin Robison Delany, *The Condition, Elevation, Emigration and Destiny of the Colored People of the United States* (New York: Arno Press and *The New York Times*, 1852, 1968); and Frederick Douglass, *Narrative of the Life of Frederick Douglass* (Garden City, NY: Anchor Books, 1845, 1963, 1973).

20. George Edward Tait, "Prerequisites for Victory in a Time of Genocide" (Harlem, NY: Unpublished transcript of lecure, 1987). Tape available from First World Alliance.

21. "No people to whom liberty is given can hold it as firmly and wear it as grandly as those who wrennch their liberty from the iron hand of the tyrant" (Frederick Douglass).

22. "We have as far as possible closed every avenue by which the light may enter the slave's mind if we could extinguish the capacty to see the light, our work would be complete. They would be then on the level with the beast of the field and we should be safe" (U.S. Senator Henry Berry speaking to the Virginia House of Delegates in 1832).

23. Arnold Hermann Ludwig Heeren, *A History of the Commerical Intercourse Between the Egyptians, the Ethiopians, and the Carthaginans* (London: D.A. Talboys, 1838).

24. George S. Schuyler, *Black and Conservative: The Autobiograhy of George S. Schuyler* (New Rochelle, NY: Arlington House, 1966).

25. John Henrik Clarke, "Chapter Eight." *Harlem School for Afrikana Studies: African Dimensions of World Culture*, Part I (Harlem, NY: Publication Pending, November 27, 1984). See also John Henrik Clarke, "Chapter Nine," *Harlem School for Afrikana Studies: African Dimensions of World Culture*, Part I (Harlem, NY: Publication Pending, December 4, 1984); James G. Frazer, *The Golden Bough: A Study in Comparative Religion* (reprinted as *The Golden Bough: The Roots of Religion and Folklore*) (New York: Avenel Books, 1890, 1981); George James Frazer, *The Folklore of the Old Testament* (New York: Crown Publishers, 1988); *Gilgamesh: A Verse Narrative*, translated by Herbert Mason with an afterword by John H. Marks (New York and Scarborough, Ontario: New American Library, 1970); Alvin Boyd Kuhn, *Who Is This King of Glory?* (Jersey City: NJ: Academy Press, 1944); Alvin Boyd Kuhn, *The Shadow of the Third Century* (Jersey City, NJ: Academy Press, 1949); Gerald Massey, *Ancient Egypt, Light of the World* (New York: Samuel Weiser, 1907); Gerald Massey, *Book of the Beginnings*, Two Volumes (Secaucus, NJ: University Books, 881, 1874); and Gerald Massey, *Gerald Massey's Lectures* (New York: Samuel Weiser, 1900).

26. John Henrik Clarke, "The Boy Who Painted Christ Black," *Opportunity Magazine* (New York: New York Urban League, 1940)).

27. "Double the gifts your mother gave you and care for her as she cared for you. She bore a heavy burden in you and did not abandon you. When she brought you forth after your months, she was still bound closely to you. For her breasts were still in your mouth for three years. While you grew, she cleaned your filth with saying, 'O, what can I do?' She placed you in school to be educated and came there daily on your behalf with bread and beer for your teacher. Thus, when you become a young man and marry a wife and establish your house, lose not sight of your own childhood. Raise your children as your mother did you. Do not let her find fault with you, lest she raise her hand to God against you and God hear her complaints and punish you" (Maulana Karenga, trans., "The Book of Ani," *Selections from the Husia: Sacred Wisdom of Ancient Egypt* (Los Angeles: Kawaida Publications, 1984), 56).

"If you are a wise man, train up a son who will be pleasing to God. If he is straight and takes after you, take good care of him. Do everything that is good for him. He is your son, your Ka begot him. Don't withdraw your heart from him. But an offspring can make trouble. If your son strays and neglects your council and disobeys all that is said, with his mouth spouting evil speech, then punish him for all his talk. God will hate him who crosses you. His guilt was determined in the womb. He who God makes boatless cannot cross the water" (Asa G. Hilliard, III; Larry Williaims, and Nia Damali, eds., *The Teachings of Ptahhotep: The Oldest Book in the World*, No. 12 (Atlanta: Blackwood Press, 1987), 22).

28. Count C.F. Volney, *The Ruins of Empire* (New York: Peter Eckler, 1789, 1802, 1890).

29. Heinrich Barth, *Travels and Discoveries in North and Central Africa*, Three Volumes (New York: Harper and Brothers,

1857). See also Lady Flora Shaw Lugard, *A Tropical Dependency* (London: James Nisbet and Co. Ltd, 1905).

30. See John Henrik Clarke's articles in the series on "Race" from *The Black American*. Series was done in early to mid-eighties.

31. According to Chief Fela Sowande, Nigerian folklorist, philosopher, educator, and concert organist and composer:

* Religion is the inner awareness of a factual dynamic relationship between the individual on one hand, and the cosmos and the world of nature on the other.

* Philosophy is the articulation of that relationship in a meaningful intelligible way, as a guide to practical living.

* Drama is the enactment of that relationship, in movement and speech.

* Art is the meaningful expression of that relationship in any medium whatsoever.

* History is the factual record of that relationship in its process of becoming; not as mere statistical facts, but as the detailed diary of the contacts between man, cosmos, and nature, room which were eventually distilled that clear awareness of the interdependence and the unbroken continuity between the three worlds.

* The science of social organization is an accurate reproduction of that same relationship, in terms of human society.

*   The science of government is the codification of that relationship and its application in that society, its purpose being to subserve the individual within the family, are determined by, and subserve, the science of government and the science of social organization (Fela Sowande, *Black Experience of Religion* (Washington, DC: Howard University Press, 1970)).

32. Sigmund Freud, *Moses and Monotheism* (London/New York: Alfred A. Knopf, 1939).

33. John Henrik Clarke, "Chapter Two: The Last Flowering of African Culture in the Western Sudan and the Assault from North Africa," *Harlem School for Afrikana Studies: African Dimensions of World Culture*, Part II (Harlem, NY: Publication Pending, April 8, 1986), 9-13. See also Felix DuBois, *Timbuctu, the Mysterious* (New York: Negro Universities Press, 1896, 1969).

34. "History is a clock people use to tell their historical, cultural, and political time of day. It's a compass that people use to find themselves on the map of human geography. History tells them where they have been, what they have been, where they are, and what they are. But most importantly, history tells a people where they still must go and what they still must be" (John Henrik Clarke).

35. "The responsibility of the writer is to make revolution irresistible" (John O. Killens).

"Suppose Russia and the United States were not at war with each other. Suppose no one is trying to fight to see which one can take over the world. Look at the energy that is being wasted that they can use. Do you know that you can build a small high school with the money that it takes to build one ballistic missile ... a high school? You can build a major college if the money wasn't being used that way; suppose it was used to benefit all of the people?"

"Look at how much better the world would be if those warring giants weren't at each other's throats and if they understood the nature of the promise they made to the world ... that they had not betrayed their revolutionary promise. One of them has betrayed their revolutionary promise just as much as the other" (John Henrik Clarke, "Chapter Three," *Harlem School for Afrikana Studies: African Dimensions of World Culture*, Part I (Harlem, NY: Publication Pending, October 23, 1984), 6)."

"Research, technology, innovation the words have taken on a crucial meaning for any nation striving for a future in a competitive world. Yet in one region, struggling to reshape itself in the most fundamental way, a dangerous practice is under way. Research is being peddled dirt cheap with dire consequences for the seller.

"Rich high-technology companies and the United States government have picked through the economic rubble of the Soviet Union to buy the skills and knowledge of the former empire's top scientists. After a lot of soul searching, the prospect of a bargain-basement price for high-tech research offset any lingering Cold War fears of financing what remains of the broken Soviet military machine.

" ... Selling science on the cheap is not the way forward for Moscow. The Soviet Union invested lost of hope and money creating one of the biggest and most advanced scientific communities in the world, teaming hundreds of researchers in pioneering institutes and now it is being let go in a desperate action.

"The money from the industrial world, however paltry, has been eagerly sought and welcomed. And why not? The alternative is unemployment or a job with a power-hungry

---

Notes   197

despot. Research jobs in the industrial world are drying up, and U.S. scientists have voiced concern about the growing exodus of experts from the former Soviet bloc competing for jobs" (From Artz, Samuel, "Anger; Price War for High-Tech Researchers," *Newsday*, 1992, 93. See also Dena Bunis, "Channel One Creator Plans Private Schools," *Newsday*, May 16, 1991, 51-52; Dona M. Richards, *Ancestor Communion: The Way to Afrikan Consciousness* (Harlem, NY: Unpublished transcript of lecture, June 3, 1989); "Rebels against the Raj: Indian Resistance against Colonial Britain during WWII," program produced by British Broadcasting Company, Cite Chandra Bose, June 12, 1990; V.T. Rajshekar, *Dalit: The Black Untouchables of India* (Atlanta/Ottawa: Clarity Press, 1987); and El-Hajj Malik Shabazz, *Malcolm X on Afro-American History* (New York: Pathfinder Press, 1967, 1970)).

Chapter Three:
THE CONTRIBUTION OF NILE VALLEY
CIVILIZATION TO WORLD CIVILIZATION

1. William H. Mackey, Jr., "History of the Arabian/Persian Gulf and Bush's War Against Iraq," a lecture delivered by William H. Mackey, Jr., December 21, 1990. See also Ralph Schoeman, *Iraq and Kuwait: A History Suppressed* (Santa Barbara, CA: Veritas Press, 1991).

2. John Henrik Clarke, "African Contribution to Early World Culture," *The African Contribution to World Culture*, Volume I (Harlem, NY: Publication Pending, 1986).

3. John Henrik Clarke, "African Culture and Universal Rise of Racism: Racism and Its Rise in the University," *The African Contribution to World Culture*, Volume II (Harlem, NY: Publication

Pending, 1986).

"Europeans were by no means the pioneers of human civilization. Half of man's recorded history had passed before anyone in Europe could read or write. The priests of Egypt began to keep written records between 4,000 and 3,000 B.C., but more than two thousand years later the poems of Homer were still being circulated in the Greek city-states by word of mouth. Shortly after 3,000 B.C., while the pharaohs were building the first pyramids, Europeans were creating nothing more distinguished than huge garbage heaps. Ironically, like pyramids, they still endure and are known to archeologists as "kitchen middens" (R.R. Palmer and Joel Colton, *A History of the Modern World* (New York: Alfred A. Knopf, 1964), 3)."

"When I was a child in school, we were taught that North America had originally been occupied by about one million Indians. That low number helped to justify the white conquest of what could then be viewed as an almost empty continent. However, archeological excavations and descriptions left by the first Europeans explorers on our coasts now suggest an initial number of around 20 million. In the century or two following Columbus's arrival it is estimated to have declined by about 95 percent.

"The man killers were European germs, to which the Indians had never been exposed and against which they therefore had neither immunologic nor genetic resistance. Smallpox, measles, influenza, and typhus competed for top rank among the killers. As if those were not enough, pertussis, plague, tuberculosis, diphtheria, mumps, malaria, and yellow fever came close behind. In countless cases Europeans were actually there to witness the decimation that occurred when the germs arrived. For example, in 1837 the Mandan Indian tribe, with one of the most elaborate cultures in the Great Plains, contracted smallpox thanks to a steamboat traveling up the

Missouri River from St. Louis. The population of one Mandan village crashed from 2,000 to less than 40 within a few weeks" (Jared Diamond, "The Arrow of Disease," *Discover Magazine*, October 1992)."

4. Jan Carew, "Columbus and the Origins of Racism in the Americas," *African Presence in the Americas: Fulcrums of Change* (Trenton, NJ: Africa World Press, Inc., 1988), 3-48. See also Bartolome De Las Casas, *The Devastation of the Indies, A Brief Account* (Baltimore/London: The Johns Hopkins University Press, 1552, 1974, 1992).

"On his second voyage to the New World in 1493, Christopher Columbus took along some hunks of sugar cane at the suggestion of Queen Isabela. In his book composed during that voyage, Peter Martyr claims the explorers found sugar cane growing in the islands of Hispaniola. Columbus suggested transporting West Indian natives to work in the Spanish sugar cane plantations. Isabella was against it. When Columbus sent two boat loads of slaves back to Spain, the Queen ordered them returned. After her death, King Ferdinand consented to recruit the first large contigent of African slaves in the burgeoning Spanish sugar industry in 1510" (William Dufty, "The Mark of Cane," *Sugar Blues* (New York: Warner Books, 1975), 32-33. See also E.D. Morel, *Red Rubber: The Story of the Rubber Slave Trade Flourishing on the Congo in the Year of Grace 1906* (New York: Negro Universities Press, 1906, 1969); Kirkpatrick Sale, *The Conquest of Paradise: Christopher Columbus and the Columbian Legacy.* (New York: Penguin Books, 1990); Eric Williams, *From Columbus to Castro, The History of the Caribbean* (New York: Vintage/Random House, 1970, 1984); and Howard Zinn, "Columbus, the Indians, and Human Progress," *A People's History of the United States* (New York: Harper/Collins, 1980, 1990)),1-22."

5. James Henry Breasted and W. Hughes Jones, *A Brief History of Ancient Times* (London: Ginn and Company Ltd, 1925, 1935, 1959), 15. See also Clinton Cox, "The Making of a Classic Myth," *The City Sun*, Brooklyn, NY, November 14-20, 1990, 8-9. Homer's accepted date has different schools of thought. Some historians place him as early as 1250 B.C., while others place him around 832 B.C. See Peter Tompkins, 1971, 1978). *Secrets of the Great Pyramid.* New York: Harper & Row.

6. E.A. Wallis Budge, *The Egyptian Book of the Dead* (The Papyrus of Ani), Egyptian text transliteration and translation (New York: Dover Publication, Inc, 1895, 1967). See also Normandi Ellis, trans., *Awakening Osiris: The Egyptian Book of the Dead* (Grand Rapids, MI: Phanes Press, 1988); and Maulana Karenga, *The Book of Coming Forth by Day: The Ethics of the Declarations of Innocence.* (Los Angeles: University of Sankore Press, 1190).

7. Richard B. Moore, *The Name "Negro": Its Origin And Evil Use.* (New York: Argentina Press, 1960).

8. Bill Keller, "Mandela, Shifting Strategy, Offers Whites an Assured Share of Power," *The New York Times*, November 20, 1992, 1.

9. Yosef A. ben-Jochannan, *We, the Black Jews: Witness to the "White Jewish Race" Myth* (New York: Alkebu-lan Books, 1984). See also Sigmund Freud, *Moses and Monotheism* (New York: Random House, 1939); Arthur Koestler, *The Thirteenth Tribe: The Khazar Empire and Its Heritage* (New York: Random House, 1976); and Joseph J. Williams, *Hebrewisms of West Africa: From Nile to Niger with the Jews* (New York: Dial Press/Toronto: Longmans, Green & Co, 1930).

10. Heinrich Barth, *Travels and Discoveries in North and Central Africa* (New York: Harper and Row, 1859). See also Leo Frobenius, *The Voice of Africa* (Salem, NH: Ayer Co. Pubs., 1913, 1991); and Arnold L. Heeren, *A History of the Commercial Intercourse Between the Egyptians the Ethiopians and the Carthaginians*, Volume IV of Heeren's historical research (London: Henry G. Bohn, 1846).

11. Maurice Delafosse, *The Negro in History (18??)*. See also Gaston Maspero, Histoire ancient des peuples d'Orient classique, Three Volumes, 12th ed. (Paris: Hachette, 1917); William M. Flinders Petrie, *Religion in Conscience in Ancient Egypt* (Salem, NH: Ayer Co. Pubs., 1898, 1991); and William M. Flinders Petrie, *Social Life in Ancient Egypt* (Boston/New York: Houghton Mifflin Co., 1923).

12. Joseph E. Harris, *Pillars in Ethiopian History: William Leo Hansberry African History Notebook*, Volume I (Washington, DC: Howard University Press, 1981). See also Joseph E. Harris, *Africa and Africans as Seen by Classical Writers: William Leo Hansberry's African History Notebook*, Volume II (Washington, DC: Howard University Press, 1981); *Herodotus, The Histories* (Middlesex, England: Penguin Books, 446 B.C., 1980); and Count C.F. Volney, 1791, *The Ruins or the Revolutions of Empires and the Laws of Nature* (New York: Peter Eckler, 1890).

13. Chancellor Williams, *The Destruction of Black Civilization, Great Issues of a Race From 4500 B.C. to 2000 A.D.* (Chicago: Third World Press, 1976), 76-91. See also Shawna Maglangbayan, *Garvey, Lumumba, Malcolm: Black Nationalist Separatists* (Chicago: Third World Press, 1972), 56-61.

14. J.A. Rogers, "Hannibal of Carthage, Father of Military Strategy," *World's Great Men of Color*, Volume I (New York: Macmillan Publishing, 1946, 1972), 98-109. See also Will Durant,

"Hannibal Against Rome: 264-202 B.C.," *The Story of Civilization*, Volume III: "Caesar and Christ" (New York: Simon and Schuster, 1944); and Mark Hyman, *Blacks Who Died for Jesus* (Philadelphia: Corrective Black History Books, 1983).

15. John G. Jackson, *Introduction to African Civilizations* (Secaucus, NJ: Citadel Press, 1970), 298-299.

16. John G. Jackson, "Africa and the Civilizing of Europe: The Empire of the Moors," *Introduction to African Civilizations* (Secaucus, NJ: Citadel Press, 1970), 157-195. See also Stanley Lane-Poole, *The Story of the Moors in Spain* (Baltimore: Black Classic Press, 1886, 1990). The Black Classic Press publication has an introduction by John G. Jackson.

17. "There are a people now forgotten (who) discovered while others were yet barbarians, the elements of the arts and sciences. A race of men now rejected for their black skin and wooly hair, founded on the study of the laws of nature those civil and religious systems which still govern the universe" (Count C.F. Volney, *The Ruins of Empires* (New York: Peter Eckler, 1793, 1890), 16-17).

18. James Adams, *Engines of War: Global Conflict, The Arms Business and the Threat to Peace* (New York: Atlantic Monthly, 1990). See also John Cook and Judith Nottingham, *A Survey of Chemical and Biological Warfare* (New York/London: Monthly Review Press, 1969).

Chapter Four:
PAN-AFRICANISM IN TRANSITION:
LOOKING TOWARD THE TWENTY-FIRST CENTURY

1. Francis Cress-Welsing, "The Concept and Color of God

and Black Mental Health," *Black Books Bulletin*, Volume 7, Number 1 (Chicago: Institute of Positive Education, 1980), 27-35.

2. Ian M. Begg, *The Cult of the Black Madonna* (London/New York: Arkana, 1985).

3. Basil Davidson, *A History of East and Central Africa to the Late Nineteenth Century* (Garden City: Doubleday/Anchor, 1967, 1969).

4. Will Durant, "VI. Cato and the Conservative Opposition," *The Story of Civilization*, Volume III: "Caesar and Christ" (New York: Simon and Schuster, 1944), 102-108. See also Clinton Cox, "Bensonhurst and the Black Italians," *The City Sun*, Brooklyn, NY, October 4-10, 1989, 26-27.

5. Stanley Lane-Poole, *The Moors in Spain* (Baltimore: Black Classic Press, 1886, 1990).

6. G.K. Osei, *Caribbean Women: Their History and Habits* (London: African Publication Society, 1979).

7. Vincent Harding, *There Is a River: The Black Struggle for Freedom in America* (New York: Harcourt Brace Jovanovich, 1981, 1983).

8. George Padmore, *Pan-Africanism, or Communism?* (Garden City, NY: Doubleday/Anchor, 1957, 1972). See also C.L.R. James, *A History of Pan-African Revolt* (Washington, DC: Drum and Spear Press, 1969).

9. John Henrik Clarke, "African Culture as a Factor in the Resistance to Slavery in the 18th Century," *African Dimensions of World Culture*, Volume II (Harlem: Publication Pending, 1986).

---

10. Picture and text from *Wonder Book*.

11. George Padmore, *Pan-Africanism, or Communism?* (Garden City, NY: Doubleday/Anchor, 1957, 1972), 119-197. See also George Padmore, ed., *History of the Pan-African Congress*, (1947, 1963), 13-23; W.E.B. DuBois, *Dusk of Dawn, An Essay Toward an Autobiography of a Race Concept* (New York: Schocken Books, 1940, 1968), 261-276; and Stephen R. Fox, *The Guardian of Boston* (New York: Atheneum, 1970).

Chapter Five:
HISTORICAL BASIS OF AFRICANCENTRICITY

1. Molefi Kete Asante, *Afrocentricity: The Theory of Social Change* (Buffalo, NY: Amulefi Publishing Company, 1980).

2. Willis N. Huggins, with John G. Jackson, *A Guide to the Study of African History* (1934). See also Willis N. Huggins, with John G. Jackson (1937), *An Introduction to African Civilization: William Leo Hansberry's African History Notebook*, Volume I: "Pillars in Ethiopian History," ed. by Joseph E. Harris (Washington, DC: Howard University Press, 1981); and William Leo Hansberry's *African History Notebook*. Volume II: "Africa and Africans as Seen by Classical Writers," ed. by Joseph E. Harris (Washington, DC: Howard University Press, 1981).

3. Proper cite on Raphael Powell. See Richard B. Moore, *The Name "Negro": It's Origin and Evil Use* (New York: Argentina Press, 1960).

4. Tony Martin, *Literary Garveyism: Garvey, Black Arts and the Harlem Renaissance* (Dover, MA: The Majority Press, 1983). See also Tony Martin, "Marcus Mosiah Garvey: Black Art

---

and the Harlem Renaissance," lecture delivered at First World Alliance, Harlem, NY, April 24, 1984. Tape available from FWA; and Daryl Cumber Dance, *Shuckin' and Jivin' Folklore from Contemporary Black Americas* (Bloomington and London: Indiana University Press, 1978).

5. The black music of the 50s showed too much devotion to black women for Macho-Macho America. James Brown epitomized the sensitivity and respect of African men towards their women when he sang "Please Don't Go."

"The Brother who could "beg" (in the tradition of Smokey, Marvin, the Dells, and many others) the best was the one who was the most popular" (Omali Yeshitela, "The Black Working Class: Reparations for Black People in the U.S.A," lecture delivered at the African Poetry Theatre, Jamaica, NY, January 8, 1984. Tape available from Afrikan American Heritage Research Center c/o African Poetry Theatre).

6. Arthur A. Schomburg, "The Negro Digs Up His Past" in Locke, Alain, ed. *The New Negro* (New York: Atheneum, 1925, 1967).

7. "The slave proved to be more skillful than the British at making cutlasses, fixing the sugar mills as wagonmasters ... at doing the basic simple work which the poor European had been brought over to do. When the slave proved to be more skillful than these poor Whites and semi-skilled Englishmen, the poor Whites lost their jobs. Then again they lost their jobs for another reason.

"The white face was at a premium. These non-status Whites were looked down on in England. Away from the homebase of England, in a sea of blackness, his whiteness meant something. Now he became a kind of small lord of the manor with property, a gun, and a white face. He had the run of the mill of the women, mostly black ones, of course.

"Many of them drank too much, gambled too much and tried to say yes to all kinds of temptation. Some of them died of just sheer physical exhaustion, but they didn't take care of business. The business that they were brought there to do was to maintain the plantation system, mechanically. When they weren't doing that then the slave had to replace them in that capacity. The Whites no longer had any usefulness on the plantation. Some of them had to go back to England; some of them died; some of them drank themselves to death. Some of them lost such little property as they had.

"The one thing the Englishman could not stand was a poor white man in the colony who brought disgrace to him on sight. He did not want the African to see poor white men running around the colony. White men, by virtue of being white, were supposed to be people of status. The English made a point of getting rid of white people without substance, visible means of support, without status and authority that commanded something.

"We see again the creation of a black craft class that could command some respect and throw some weight around. We see the pressure that made the Caribbean slave system one of the worst in the hemisphere . . . we see it lighten. At first slaves were sent to the Caribbean or left in the Caribbean to be broken for the American slave market. They were broken just as you tame horses for use. However, that had to stop once there was a semblance of power and authority that fell into the hands of a black craft class who controlled something. They began to control something to the point where the Caribbean freeman and the black freeman in the United States began to interact and correspond with each other" (Harlem School For African Studies. Course: African Contribution to World Culture. Part II. Instructor: Dr. John Henrik Clarke. Session Seven: "African Culture as a Factor in the Resistance to Slavery in the 18th Century," May 20,

1986. Unpublished Transcript).

8. C.L.R. James, *The Black Jacobins: Toussaint L'Ouverture and the San Domingo Revolution* (New York: Random House, 1963). See also Eric Williams, *From Columbus to Castro: The History of the Caribbean* (New York: Random House, 1984); and Jacob H. Carruthers, *The Irritated Genie: An Essay on the Haitian Revolution* (Chicago: The Kemetic Institute, 1985).

9. Vincent Harding, *There Is a River: The Black Struggle for Freedom in America* (New York: Harcourt Brace Jovanovich, 1981). See also Paula Gidding, *When and Where I Enter* (New York: Morrow, 1984).

10. Edward Scobie, "Afrikan Consciousness and White Supremacy Domination," Harlem, NY: Unpublished Lecture, June 17, 1989. Audiotape "Afrikan Literary Consciousness in the Diaspora, 1750-1850," Harlem, NY: Unpublished Lecture, June 1, 1991. Audiotape available from First World Alliance; Harlem, NY.

11. Edward Wilmot Blyden, "The Aims and Methods of a Liberal Education for Africans, Inaugural Address as President of Liberia College, delivered at Monrovia, 5 January 1881," *Christianity, Islam and the Negro Race* (Edinburgh: Edinburgh University Press, 1967). See also Hollis R. Lynch, *Edward Wilmot Blyden: Pan-Negro Patriot, 1832-1922* (London/Oxford/New York: Oxford Univeristy Press, 1967).

12. J.A. Rogers, *World's Great Men of Color*, "Introduction" by John Henrik Clarke, Volume I (New York: Macmilan, 1946, 1972), ix-xvi. See also J.A. Rogers, "Mohammed Ahmed—The Mahdi: Conqueror of the Great English General Gordon," *World's Great Men of Color*, Volume I (New York: Macmillan, 1946, 1972), 295-309; J.A. Rogers, "Mohammed Abdullah—The Mad Mullah."

World's Great Men of Color, Volume II (New York: Macmillan, 1947, 1972), 543; and E.A.Ayandele, *Holy Johnson: Pioneer of African Nationalism, 1835-1917* (London: Frank Cass & Co., Ltd., 1970).

13. W.E.B. Du Bois, *The Suppression of the African Slave Trade to the United States of America, 1638-1870* (New York: Longmans, Green and Co., 1897). See also W.E.B. Du Bois, *The Philadelphia Negro: A Social Study* (Philadelphiia: University of Pennsylvania, 1899); W.E.B. Du Bois, *The Souls of Balck Folk: Essays and Sketches* (Chicago: A.C. McClurg and Co., 1903); W.E.B. Dubois, *The Gift of Black Folk: Negroes in the Making of America* (Boston: TheStratford Co., 1924); W.E.B. Du Bois, *Black Reconstruction in America, 1860-1880*, published by the editors of Freedomways. (1970) and edited by John Henrik Clarke, Esther Jackson, Ernest Kaiser, and J.H. O'Dell (Boston: Beacon Press, 1935).

14. James Baldwin, *Go Tell It On The Mountain* (New York: Dell Publishing Co., 1952). See also John Blassingame, *The Slave Community: Plantation Life in the Antebellum South* (New York: Oxford University Press, 1972, 1979); Sterling Stuckey, *Slave Culture: Nationalist Theory and the Foundations of Black America* (New York: Oxford University Press, 1988); and Margaret Walker, *Jubilee* (New York: Bantam, 1975).

Chapter Six:
EDUCATION FOR A NEW REALITY
IN THE AFRICAN WORLD

1. "History is a clock people use to tell their historical culture and political time of the day. It's a compass that people use to find themselves on the map of human geography. The history tells them where they have been, where they are and what they

---

are. But most importantly history tells a people where they still must go and what they still must be (John Henrik Clarke)."

"The best way to effectively fight an alien culture is to live our own" (Haki R. Madhubuti, *The Book of Life* (Chicago: The Institute of Positive Education, 1973)).

2. " ... Thus it was on the edges of our continent—where some of us gulped down handfuls of sand in a last effort to hold the reality of the land—that the long struggle for black freedom began" (Vincent Harding, *There is a River: The Black Struggle for Freedom in Black America* (New York: Harcourt Brace Jovanovich, 1981), 3).

3. "We have to realize that education has but one honorable purpose ... one alone ... everything else is a waste of time: that is to train the student to be a proper handler of power. Being Black and beautiful means nothing until ultimately you're Black and powerful. The world is ruled by power, not blackness and not beauty.

"If the day comes when fate is so cruel that it will let the meek inherit the earth .. the strong are going to inherit the meek and the status quo is going to remain the same. And powerful people never educate powerless people in what they need that they can use to take the power away from powerful people; it's too much to expect. If I was in power I would not educate people in how to take my power away from me" (John Henrik Clarke, "Like It Is" (WABC Public Affairs Television), New York: Capitol Cities Broadcasting, taped: July 2, 1992, Airdate: July 12, 1992. Transcript available from Journal Graphics, Denver, CO).

"Those who profess to favor freedom yet deprecate agitation are men who want crops without plowing up the ground; they want rain without thunder and lightning. They want the ocean without the awful roar of its many waters.

"This struggle may be a moral one, or it may be a physical one, and it may be both moral and physical, but it must be a struggle. *Power concedes nothing without a demand. It never did and it never will. Find out just what any people will quietly submit to and you have found out the exact measure of injustice and wrong which will be imposed upon them, and these will continue till they are resisted with either words or blows, or with both. The limits of tyrants are prescribed by the endurance of those whom they oppress.*

" ... Men may not get all they pay for in this world, but they certainly must pay for all they get. If we ever get free from the oppressions and wrongs heaped upon us, we must pay for their removal. We must do this by labor, by suffering, by sacrifice, and if needs be, by our lives and the lives of others" (Frederick Douglass, "West India Day Emancipation," speech delivered at Canandaigua, NY, in 1857 in Philip S. Foner, ed., *The Life and Writings of Frederick Douglass*, Volume II: "Pre-civil War Decade, 1850-1860" (New York: International Publishers, 1950), 437. Emphasis added.

4. Vincent Harding, *There is a River: The Black Struggle for Freedom in America* (New York. Harcourt, Brace Jovanovich, 1981).

5. Lerone Bennett, "Father of the Protest Movement: Frederick Douglass," *Pioneers in Protest* (Chicago: Johnson Publishing Co., 1968), 197-217. See also Lerone Bennett, "Nay-Sayer of the Black Revolt: Henry Highland Garnett," *Pioneers in Protest* (Chicago: Johnson Publishing Co., 1968), 149-158; Lerone Bennett, "Guerrilla in the Cottonfields: Harriet Tubman," *Pioneers in Protest* (Chicago: Johnson Publishing Co., 1968), 115-128; John H. Bracey, Jr., August Meier, and Elliott Rudwick, *Black National-ism in America* (Indianapolis: Bobbs-Merrill Educational Publishing, 1970); Benjamin Brawley, *Negro Builders and Heroes*

(Chapel Hill: The University of North Carolina Press, 1937), 61-66; Anna Julia Cooper, *A Voice From the South* (Oxford/New York: Oxford University Press, 1892); *Martin Robison Delany, the Condition, Elevation, Emigration and Destiny of the Colored People of the United States* (New York: Arno Press and the New York Times, 1852, 1968); *Frederick Douglass, Narrative of the Life of Frederick Douglass* (Garden City, NY: Anchor/Doubleday, 1845, 1963); Philip S. Foner, *The Voice of Black America: Major Speeches by Negroes in the United States 1797-1900*, Volume I (New York: Capricorn Books, 1972); Vincent Harding, *There Is A River: The Black Struggle for Freedom in America* (New York: Harcourt Brace Jovanovich, 1981); and J.A. Rogers, "Frederick Douglass: Ex-Slave Who Rose to Be A Mighty Champion," *World's Great Men of Color*, Volume II (New York: Macmillan Publishing, 1947, 1972), 332-349.

6. J.A. Rogers, "Dom Pedro II, The Magnanimous," *World's Great Men of Color*, Volume II (New York: Macmillan Publishing, 1947, 1972), 203-214. See also Yusef Abdul Salaam, *Capoeira: African Brazilian Karate* (Harlem, NY: Self-published, 1983) and "Quilombo," a film by Carlos Dieques, Brazilian film maker.

7. Lerone Bennett, *Before the Mayflower: A History of Black America* (Chicago: Johnson Publishing Co., 1961). See also Lerone Bennett, "Colonial Catalyst: Prince Hall," *Pioneers in Protest* (Chicago: Johnson Publishing Co, 1968), 29-39; Lerone Bennett, "Founders of the Black Press: Samuel E. Comish and John B. Russwurm," *Pioneers in Protest* (Chicago: Johnson Publishing Co., 1960), 59-66; Walter Rodney, *A History of the Guyanese Working People, 1881-1905* (Baltimore: John Hopkins University, 1981); Walter Rodney, *A History of the Upper Guinea Coast 1545-1800* (Boston: Monthly Review Press, 1980); and Walter Rodney, *How Europe Underdeveloped Africa* (Washington, DC: Howard Unviersity Press, 1982).

8. Edward Wilmot Blyden, *The Aims and Methods of a Liberal Education for Africans*, "Inaugural Address," delivered by Edward Wilmot Blyden, President of Liberia College, January 5, 1881, *Christianity, Islam and the Negro Race* (Edinburgh: Edinburgh University Press, 1967); See also Hollis R. Lynch, *Edward Wilmot Blyden: Pan-Negro Patriot, 1832-1912* (New York: Oxford University Press, 1967).

9. "Meanwhile for several centuries, there had been a steady movement into Hausa lands of a pastoral tribe, the Fulani of whose origin little is known. While most of the Fulani remained with their herds, moving from place to place in search of water and pasturage, a number drifted to the towns and mingled with the Hausa population. Their intelligence and ability quickly established these 'town Fulani' in a position of influence.
"Such a position had been gained by Usman (Othman) dan Fodio, a Fulani sheikh of great reputed sanctity who had made the pilgrimage to Mecca. When, about 1802, Usman intervened on behalf of a number of Muslims who had been enslaved, the King Gobir ordered his arrest and Usman roused his followers to revolt. Recognized as Sarkin Musulmi (commander of the Faithful), Usman was supported by the Fulani and some of the Muslim Hausa and easily defeated the forces of Gobir, later conquering all the Hausa lands in a triumphant jihad, which was directed agaisnt lax or lukewarm Muslims and paans (traditional worship)" (Encyclopaedia Britannica, Volume XVI: "Nigeria" (Chicago: The University of Chicago, 1969), 502).

10. Francis Cress Welsing, "The Concept of the Color of God and Black Mental Health," *Black Books Bulletin*, Volume 7, Number 1 (Chicago: Insitute of Positive Education, 1980). See also Bishop Henry McNeil Turner, "God is a Negro," *Voice of Missions* (1898), reprinted in *Black Nationalism in America*, edited by John H. Bracey, Jr, August Meier, and Elliott Rudwick (Indianapolis:

Bobbs-Merrill Educational Publications, 1970), 154-155.

11. Alexander Crummell, "Civilization: The Primal Need of Our Race," *OCCASIONAL PAPERS No. 3* (Washington, DC: The AmericanNegro Academy (1897), reprinted in *Black Nationalism in America,* edited by John H. Bracey, Jr., August Peier, and Elliott Rudwick (Indianapolis: Bobbs-Merrill Educational Publications, 1970)), 139-143.

12. "For a while it looked as though Oklahoma might become a place of safety for Black Americans. Boley, with its eight acres and four thousand residents, boasted the tallest building between Oklahoma City and Okmulgee. More important, it could state that black people ran the government and that half of its high school students went on to college. Boley often struck an independent note, as when its "Union Literary Society" debated the question whether Blacks should "celebrate George Washington's birthday," and decided in the negative." See also William Loren Katz, *The Black West* (Garden City, NY: Doubleday, 1971), 250.

13. Booker T. Washington, *Up From Slavery* (New York: Al Bert Company, 1901). See also Booker T. Washington, *My Work* (Garden City, NY: Doubleday, 1911).

14. "If you read the speech you'll find out that the speech is many things to many people. There are many things that went unnoticed. Now I had a habit of almost twenty years of reading the speech once a year and I got something different out of the speech each year.
"He didn't come back and change the speech and nobody changed the punctuation marks: why did I get something different out of the speech each year. . . and grow more respectful toward the speech year by year? I have grown

intellectually year by year and I understand the bind he was in . . .and the games he had to play in order to survive. Now that does not mean I agree with all of them, but I understood that he had to play certain games.

"Now, in the speech, he appealed to the South, the North, the Blacks, and the Whites. He was saying that it is better to make a dollar a day than to sit next to a white man at an opera. This was interpreted as meaning he did not agree with social equality. It's not what Booker T. Washington said . . . it's what the white editors interpreted him as having said.

"When he said it's better to own a truck farm than to be out political stump speaking that was interpreted as meaning that he agreed with the disenfranchisement of the black voter. This injustice was done to him by Whites who misinterpreted what he was trying to say. What he was saying was first things first. Take care your house; take care of your family; learn a basic skill; if you're going to be a servant, be a good servant and demand a better price for it.

"Although the speech was in 1895, most of the Jim Crow laws came into being in the years between 1895 and 1900 as a result of the misinterpretations of that speech. Now you could understand why a generation of Blacks who didn't understand him, or his speech, would call him Uncle Tom and Compromiser. He didn't compromise, others compromised him. We could not distinguish between the victim and those who had victimized the victim" (John Henrik Clarke, "The Impact of African Culture on the Twentieth Century," *Harlem School for Afrikana Studies; African Dimensions of World Culture*, Part II, June 10, 1986, Chapter Ten, pp. 2-3).

15. George Breitman, "Message to the Grassroots." *Malcolm X Speaks* (New York: Grove Press, Inc, 1965), 4-17.

16. Mari Evans, "Speak the Truth to the People," *I Am A Black Woman* (New York: William Morrow and Co., 1970).

"We have as far as possible closed every avenue by which the light may enter the slave's mind—if we could extinguish the capacity to see the light our work would be complete. They would then be on the level with the beast of the field and we should be safe" (U.S. Senator Henry Berry, 1832, Addressing Virginia House of Delegates).

17. Pauli Murray, *Southern Magazine*. Lillian Smith, ed., (c. 1970).

18. Special issue of *Nommo*.

19. Margaret Walker, *For My People* (New Haven, CT: Yale University Press, 1942).

Bibliography

Bardolph, Richard. 1959. *The Negro Vanguard.* New York: Rinehart.

ben-Jochannan,Yosef A.A. 1971. *Africa: Mother of Western Civilization.* Alkebulan Books, c/o Dr. Arthur Lewis, 725 St. Nicholas Ave., New York, 10030.

_____ . 1978. *Our Back Seminarians and Black Clergy Without a Black Theology.* New York: Alkebulan Books and Education Materials Associates.

_____ . 1983. *We the Black Jews,* Vol. I and II. New York: Alkebu-lan Books.

Bennett, Lerone. 1984. *Before the Mayflower.* New York: Penguin Books.

Betts, Raymond E. 1966. *The Scramble for Africa: Causes and Dimensions of Empire.* Boston: Heath and Co.

Blyden, Edward Wilmot. 1967. *Christianity, Islam and the Negro Race.* Edinburgh: Edinburgh University Press.

Bontemps, Arna. 1972. *The Harlem Renaissance Remembered.* New York: Dodd Mead.

Breitman, George, ed. 1965. *Malcolm X, the Man and His Ideas,* A Speech Delivered to the Friday Night Socialist Forum at Eugene V. Debs Hall in Detroit on March 5, 1965. New York: Pioneer Publishers.

_____, ed. 1967. *The Last Year of Malcolm X The Evolution of a Revolutionary*, New York: Pathfinder Press.

_____, ed. 1970. *By Any Means Necessary, Speeches, Interviews and a Letter by Malcolm X.* New York: Pathfinder Press.

Breitman, George, Herman Porter and Baxter Smith. 1976. *The Assassination of Malcolm X.* New York: Pathfinder Press.

Brotz, Howard, ed. 1966. *Social and Political Thought, 1850-1920.* New York: Basic Books, Inc.

Carmichael, Stokely and Charles Hamilton. 1967. *Black Power.* New York: Random House.

Clarke, John H., ed. 1970. *Black Titan: W.E.B. Du Bois.* Boston: Beacon Press.

Cox, Richard. 1982. *The Ideology of Pan-African Scientific Communalism.* Sussex, Sierra Leone, West Africa.

_____. 1964. *Pan-Africanism in Practice, An East African Study.* London: Oxford University Press.

Davidson, Basil. 1973. *Black Star: A View of the Life and Times of Kwame Nkrumah.* New York: Praeger Publishers.

Davis, Lenwood G. and Janet L. Sims, compilers. 1980. *Marcus Garvey, An Annotated Bibliography,* Foreword by John Henrik Clarke. Westport, CN: Greenwood Press.

De Graft-Johnson. 1954. *African Glory, The Story of Vanished Negro Civilizations.* Toronto: George J. McLeod, Limited.

Diop, Cheikh Anta. 1974. *The African Origins of Civilizations: Myth or Reality.* Westport, CN: Lawrence Hill & Co.

_____ . 1960. *Black Africa: The Economic and Cultural Bases of A Federated State.* Paris: Presence Africaine.

_____ . 1989. *Civilization or Barbarism.* Westport, CN: Lawrence Hill and Co.

Drake, St. Clair. 1971. *The Redemption of Africa and Black Religion.* Chicago: Third World Press.

Drimmer, Melvin, ed. 1969. *Black History, A Reappraisal.* New York: Doubleday Anchor Books.

Du Bois, W.E.B. 1968. *The Autobiography of W.E.B. Du Bois.* New York: International Publisher.

_____ . 1968. *Dusk of Dawn, An Essay Toward An Autobiography of A Race Concept.* New York: Schocken Book.

Esedebe, P. Olisanwuche. 1982. *Pan-Africanism The Idea and Movement 1776-1963.* Washington, DC: Howard University Press.

Essien-Udom, E.U. 1964. *Black Nationalism: A Search for an Identity in America.* New York: Dell Publishing Co.

Fitch, Bob and Oppenheimer, Mary. July-August 1966. *GHANA: End of an Illusion.* New York: Monthly Review Press, Vol. 18, Number 3.

Foner, Eric, ed. 1970. *America's Black Past, A Reader in Afro-American History.* New York: Harper and Row.

Franklin, John Hope. 1980. *From Slavery to Freedom: A History of Negro Americans.* New York: Alfred A. Knopf (fiifth ed.).

_____ . 1985. *George Washington Williams, A Biography.* Chicago: University of Chicago Press.

Garvey, Amy Jacques. 1962. *Garvey and Garveyism.* Jamaica, W.I.: United Printers Ltd. 218 Marcus Garvey Drive, Kingston 11.

_____, compiler. 1967. *The Philosophy and Opinions of Marcus Garvey or Africa for the Africans*, With a New Introduction by E.U. Essien-Udom, Two Volumes in One. London: Frank Cass.

Garvey, Amy Jacques and E.U. Essien-Uldom, eds. 1977. *More Philosophy and Opinions of Marcus Garvey*, Vol. 3. London: Frank Cass.

Grant, Joanne, 1968. *Black Protest: History, Documents and Analysis, 1619 to the Present.* Edited with introduction and commentary by Joanne Grant, Greenwich, CA: Fawcet Premier Books.

Graves, Robert and Patai, Raphael. 1963. *Hebrew Myths: The Books of Genesis*, New York: McGraw Hill.

Guillaume, Alfred. 1981. *Islam.* Baltimore: Penguin Books.

Hansberry, William Leo. 1963. "Africa, World's Richest Continent,/ New York: Freedomways, Winter.

_____ . 1981. *African History Notebook*. Volumes I: Pillars in Ethiopian History and II: Africa and Africans as Seen by Classical Writers. Washington, DC: Howard University Press.

Harding, Vincent. 1981. *There Is a River, The Black Struggle for Freedom in America.* New York: Harcourt, Brace, Jovanovich.

Hill, Rovert A, ed. 1987. *Marcus Garvey Life and lessons, A Centennial Companion to the Marcus Garvey and Universal Negro Improvement Association Papers.* Berkeley and Los Angeles, CA: University of California Press.

_____ . 1983-1989. *The Marcus Garvey and Universal Negro Improvement Association Papers*, Vols. 1-7 (A Projected 8 Volumes). Berkeley: University of California Press.

Hooker, James R. 1967. *Black Revolutionary George Padmore's Path from Communism to Pan-Africanism.* New York: Frederick A Praeger, Inc.

_____. 1975. Henry Sylvester Williams, *Imperial Pan-Africanist.* London: Rex Collings, Ltd.

Jackson, John G. 1974. *Introduction to African Civilizations.* Secaucus, N.J: The Citadel Press.

James, C.L.R. 1977. *Nkrumah and the Ghana Revolution.* Westport, CN: Lawrence Hill and Co.

Karim, Imam Benjamin, ed. 1971. *The End of White World Supremacy, Four Speeches by Malcolm X.* New York: Merlin House.

King, Martin Luther, Jr. 1958. *Stride Toward Freedom, The Montgomery Story.* New York: Ballantine Books.

Kritzeck, James and Lewis, William H, eds. 1969. *Islam in Africa.* New York: Van Nostrand-Reinhold Company.

Langley, J. Ayoodele. 1973. *Pan-Africanism and Nationalism in West Africa 1900-1945.* New York: Oxford University Press.

Lardolph, Richard. 1961. *The Negro Vanguard.* New York: Vintage.

Latham, Frank B. 1969. *The Rise and Fall of "Jim Crow,/ 1865-1964.* New York: F. Watts.

Legum, Colin. 1962. *Pan-Africanism A Short Political Guide.* NY: Praeger Paperbacks.

Lemarchand, Rene. 1964. *Political Awakening in the Belgian Congo.* Berkeley and Los Angeles: University of California Press.

Lewis, Rupert and Warner-Lewis, Maureen. 1986. *Garvey, Africa, Europe, the Americas.* Kingston, Jamaica: The Herald, Ltd.

Logan, Rayford. 1961. *The Betrayal of the Negro from Rutherford B. Hayes to Woodrow Wilson.* New York: Collier Books.

Lomax, Louis. 1968. *To Kill A Black Man.* Los Angeles: Holloway House.

Lynch, Hollis R. 1966. "Pan-Negro Nationalism in the New World Before 1862./ *African History.* Ed. by Jeffrey Butler. Vol. II. Boston: Boston University Press papers on Africa.

McAdoo, Bill. 1983. *Pre-Civil War Black Nationalism.* New York: The David Walker Press.

Madhubuti, Haki R. 1978. *Enemies: The Clash of Races.* Chicago: Third World Press.

Majeke, Nosipho. 1952. *The Role of the Missionary in Conquest.* Johannesburg, South Africa: Johannesburg Society of Young Africa.

Malcolm X. 1964. *The Autobiography.* With the assistance of Alex Haley. New York: Grove Press.

_____. 1969. "Malcolm X Talks to Young People," New York: A Young Socialist Pamphlet.

_____. 1970. *On Afro-American History.* Expanded and Illustrated Edition. New York: Pathfinder Press.

Martin, Tony. 1983. *The Pan-African Connection: From Slavery to Garvey and Beyond.* Dover, MA: The Majority Press.

_____. 1976. *Race First, The Ideological and Organizational Struggles of Marcus Garvey and the Universal Negro Improvement Association.* Westport, CN: Greenwood Press.

_____ , ed. 1986. *Marcus Garvey, Message to the People, the Course of African Philosophy*. Dover, MA: The Majority Press.

Mazrui, Ali. 1986. *The Africans. A Triple Heritage*. Boston: Little, Brown and Co.

Mazrui, Ali and Robert I. Rotberg, eds. 1970. *Protest and Power in Black Africa*. New York: Oxford University Press.

Meredith, Martin. 1984. *The First Dance of Freedom, Black Africa in the Post-war Era*. New York: Oxford University Press.

Nkrumah, Kwame. 1963. *Africa Must Unite*. New York: Frederick A. Praeger.

_____ . 1968. *Dark Days in Ghana*. New York: International Publishers.

_____ .1965. *Neocolonialism, The Last Stage of Imperialism*. New York: International Publishers.

Okumu, Washington. 1963. *Lumumba's Congo: Roots of Conflict*. New York: Ivan Obolensky.

Walters, Ronald. 1987. "White Racial Nationalism in the United States." *Without Prejudice*. Washington, DC: The EAFORD International Review of Racial Discrimination. vol. I, No. I, Fall.

Webster, J.B. and A.A. Boahen and H.O. Idowuy. 1970. *The Growth of African Civilization: The Revolutionary Years: West Africa Since 1800*. New York: Praeger.